The Empathy Garden: Growing Kindness & Understanding in Young Minds

Time to Sign
Play to Learn Series

Table of Contents

Chapter 1
Introduction: The Concept of the Empathy Garden

Welcome to "The Concept of the Empathy Garden" — a guide designed for early childhood social-emotional educators. This book is an exploration into the world of empathy, tailored to the fertile minds of young learners. As an educator, you are familiar with the importance of nurturing not just the intellect, but also the heart. In these pages, we present the Empathy Garden: a metaphorical and practical space where empathy can be cultivated, grown, and harvested among children.

Empathy, the ability to understand and share the feelings of others, is a crucial skill for social and emotional development. However, teaching empathy to young children requires more than just talking about feelings. It requires a tangible, engaging, and interactive approach. This is where the Empathy Garden comes into play.

The Empathy Garden is not just a physical space but a framework for educational experiences. It's a conceptual garden where emotions, thoughts, and interpersonal skills are planted, cared for, and grown. Just like seeds in a garden, each child's empathetic abilities require nurturing, patience, and the right environment to flourish. Throughout this book, we will explore various methods and activities to create and maintain your Empathy Garden.

You'll learn how to:

- **Plant the Seeds of Empathy:** Introduce the concept of empathy through stories, role-playing, and discussions.
- **Cultivate Emotional Literacy:** Help children identify, express, and understand their own emotions and those of others.
- **Grow Compassionate Actions:** Guide children in developing kindness, understanding, and positive interactions with their peers.
- **Harvest Reflective Thoughts:** Encourage children to reflect on their actions and the feelings of others, fostering a deeper sense of empathy.

Remember, every child's emotional landscape is unique. The Empathy Garden approach is flexible, allowing you to tailor activities and discussions to the needs of your students. This book is not just a teaching tool; it's a journey into the heart of early childhood education. Together, let's cultivate a generation of empathetic, understanding, and emotionally intelligent individuals. Welcome to the Empathy Garden — let's start planting!

Introduce the Metaphor of a Garden to Explain Empathy

Welcome, educators, to a journey through the Empathy Garden, a metaphorical landscape where the seeds of understanding and compassion are sown in the hearts of young children. As an educator in the field of early childhood social-emotional behavior(s), you understand the profound impact of nurturing empathy in the early years of development. This book is your guide to cultivating these essential skills using the rich and engaging metaphor of a garden.

The Empathy Garden represents the fertile ground of a child's emotional and social landscape, where empathy can be planted, nurtured, and grown. Like a garden, empathy requires careful tending and the right conditions to flourish. The soil represents the supportive environment you provide, the seeds are the lessons of compassion and understanding, the water is the ongoing encouragement and reinforcement, and the sunlight is the love and positive role modeling they see in you.

In this introduction, we will explore:

- **The Soil** – Preparing the Ground: How to create a nurturing and safe emotional environment in your classroom that encourages openness and trust.
- **Planting the Seeds** – Introducing Empathy: Techniques to introduce the concept of empathy to young children in a way that is understandable and relatable.
- **Watering the Seedlings** – Encouraging Empathetic Growth: Strategies to help children recognize and respond to their own emotions and those of others, reinforcing empathetic behaviors.
- **Basking in the Sunlight** – Leading by Example: How your actions, as an educator, serve as a model for empathetic behavior, much like sunlight helps a garden grow.
- **Harvesting the Blooms** – Celebrating Empathy: Recognizing and celebrating acts of empathy in the classroom, reinforcing these important behaviors.

By using the Empathy Garden metaphor, we can help young children grasp the abstract concept of empathy in a tangible and relatable way. This book aims to provide you with the tools and strategies to cultivate a generation of empathetic, compassionate, and socially aware individuals. Let's begin our journey through the Empathy Garden and watch as empathy blooms in the hearts and minds of our young learners.

Nurturing Empathy - A Journey from Seed to Blossom

Welcome, educators and guides in the vital journey of nurturing young minds. This book is a tribute to your role in cultivating empathy in early childhood, a journey akin to growing a beautiful, thriving garden. Just as a gardener tends to a plant, helping it grow from a tiny seed into a flourishing bloom, you nurture the seed of empathy in young children, guiding its growth and development through the various stages of their early years.

Empathy, the ability to understand and share the feelings of another, is not an innate fully-formed attribute but rather a quality that develops and deepens over time, much like a growing plant. This book is crafted to guide you through this process of nurturing empathy in children, using the metaphor of a plant's growth to illustrate its development.

The Stages of Empathy's Growth:

1. **Planting the Seed** - Introducing Empathy: Just as a garden begins with a seed, the journey of empathy starts with introducing the concept to children. This stage is about laying the foundation by discussing feelings and the importance of understanding others.
2. **Germination** - Awakening Awareness: As a seed germinates, it begins to sprout and grow. Similarly, children start to become aware of their own emotions and begin to recognize that others have feelings too.
3. **Rooting** - Deepening Understanding: A plant's roots anchor it and help it absorb nutrients. In this stage, children's understanding of empathy deepens. They learn to see things from others' perspectives and to understand that everyone's feelings are important.
4. **Stem and Leaves** - Growing Skills: As a plant's stem and leaves grow, it gains strength. Children develop stronger empathy skills, such as active listening and compassion, and begin to respond more effectively to the feelings of others.
5. **Flowering** - Demonstrating Empathy: The flowering stage is the culmination of a plant's growth, just as the demonstration of empathy in actions and words is the culmination of its development in children. Here, empathy is fully expressed as children show genuine concern and kindness towards others.

Throughout this book, we will explore each stage in detail, providing you with strategies, activities, and insights to help you nurture empathy in children. Remember, just like plants, each child grows at their own pace and in their own way. Your role is to provide the care, support, and the environment necessary for this growth.

Let's embark on this journey together, nurturing the seeds of empathy in the fertile soil of young hearts and minds, watching as they grow into compassionate, understanding individuals.

Chapter II
Planting the Seeds of Empathy

The Importance of Empathy:

The Fertile Ground of Early Childhood

The process of fostering empathy commences in the vibrant and fertile terrain of early childhood. This phase represents a period of significant development, wherein each interaction and experience serve as a chance to cultivate the seeds of empathy in young minds. Whether you are an educator or caregiver, you possess the tools to delicately cultivate this soil, priming it for the invaluable lessons of kindness, understanding, and emotional connection.

Understanding Empathy in Young Children

Empathy is often thought of as a single skill, but in young children, it's a complex tapestry woven from several strands of development: emotional awareness, perspective-taking, and compassionate action. At this tender age, empathy starts as a basic awareness of others' emotions and gradually evolves into understanding, feeling with, and responding to these emotions in a caring manner.

Emotional Mirroring: The First Sprouts of Empathy

In the initial phases, the development of empathy initiates through emotional mirroring. Children observe and mirror the emotions displayed by others, laying the groundwork for a more profound comprehension. Within your Empathy Garden, take note of how children respond to diverse emotional situations. Are they visibly worried when a peer is distressed? Do they reciprocate with smiles when you express happiness? These initial manifestations are the first sprouts of empathy, indicating a readiness for further guided exploration of emotions.

Sowing the Seeds: Activities for Empathy Development

Engaging young children in empathy-building activities is like planting seeds in well-prepared soil.

Here are a few activities to start with:

1. **Storytime with a Heart:** Choose stories that highlight emotions and ask open-ended questions like, "How do you think the character feels?" This encourages children to think about and articulate emotions.

2. **Emotion Charades:** Use facial expressions and body language to express various emotions, encouraging children to guess the feelings you are conveying. This activity aids in their development of the ability to interpret and comprehend emotional cues.

3. **Empathy in Action:** Model empathetic behavior in your interactions. When a child experiences a strong emotion, acknowledge it and show understanding. This demonstrates empathy in action, a powerful lesson for young minds.

The Role of Consistency and Patience

Like any garden, the Empathy Garden requires consistent care and patience. Empathy doesn't bloom overnight. It develops through repeated exposure to understanding and compassionate interactions. Celebrate small moments of empathetic behavior and reflect on them with the children, reinforcing the value of understanding and caring for others.

Conclusion

Sowing the seeds of empathy during early childhood lays the foundation for a lifetime characterized by emotional intelligence and social connectivity. When you actively participate in empathetic practices, promote emotional understanding, and exemplify compassionate behavior, you are not merely imparting a skill; you are cultivating a future marked by empathy and understanding.

Activities and Stories to Cultivate Empathy

Crafting the Roots of Empathy Through Storytelling

One of the most powerful tools in cultivating empathy in young children is storytelling. Stories have a unique way of engaging children's emotions and imagination, making them ideal for illustrating empathy in simple, relatable terms.

Activity: The Story Circle

Create a story circle where each child gets a turn to share a story about a time they felt a strong emotion – happy, sad, scared, or angry. After each story, discuss as a group how they might have felt, emphasizing the importance of listening and understanding each other's feelings. This activity not only fosters empathy but also builds a sense of community and belonging in the classroom.

Featured Story: "The Little Cloud That Cried"

In this story, a little cloud feels left out and starts to cry, causing a downpour. The sun asks why the cloud is crying and tries to understand its feelings. Eventually, the sun helps the cloud see how its tears help the plants and animals, turning its sadness into joy. This simple story helps children understand that empathizing with others' feelings can lead to positive outcomes and shared happiness.

Interactive Empathy: Role-Playing Games

Role-playing is an effective way to teach empathy. By putting themselves in someone else's shoes, children can better understand different perspectives and emotions.

Activity: Emotion Role-Play

Set up scenarios where children have to act out different emotions and situations. For instance, one child pretends to be a character who has lost their toy, while others respond. Discuss afterwards how each child felt during the role-play, emphasizing the importance of considering others' feelings in their responses.

Empathy Through Art: Expressing Emotions Creatively

Art offers a non-verbal way for children to express and understand emotions, an essential aspect of empathy.

Activity: Emotion Collage
Provide various art materials like colored paper, markers, and magazines for children to create a collage about different emotions. Let them choose an emotion to depict and then share their collage with the group, explaining why they chose certain images or colors. This activity helps children understand that emotions can be complex and personal, yet shared and understood by others.

Conclusion: The Foundation of Empathetic Understanding
These activities and stories are just the beginning of planting the seeds of empathy. By regularly incorporating these into your curriculum, you help children understand and express emotions, paving the way for deeper empathetic connections. Remember, each activity is an opportunity to water and nurture these seeds, gradually growing a garden rich with kindness and understanding.

Ten Stories to Nurture Empathy:

1. "The Lonely Frog"
A little frog feels lonely because he's different from his peers. A kind turtle decides to befriend him, showing that understanding and acceptance can bridge differences.

2. "The Bear Who Shared"
A bear has a big pile of berries and learns the joy of sharing with others who have none. This story highlights how empathy leads to generous actions.

3. "The Elephant Who Listened"
An elephant uses its big ears to listen to the problems of other animals in the jungle, teaching the value of being a good listener and understanding others' perspectives.

4. "The Kitten's New Friend"
A kitten befriends a scared puppy who has just moved into the neighborhood. The kitten helps the puppy feel at home, showcasing empathy in welcoming new friends.

5. "The Little Cloud's New Perspective"
A cloud always rains on a parade until it understands how its actions affect the people below. This story is about understanding the impact of our actions on others.

6. "Mia's First Day"
Mia is nervous on her first day at a new school, but a classmate helps her feel welcome. This story illustrates empathy by understanding and alleviating someone's fears.

7. "The Ant and the Dove"
An ant and a dove help each other in times of need, showing that acts of kindness are often reciprocated and appreciated.

8. "The Tree That Gave Shelter"
A generous tree offers shelter to various animals, teaching the importance of helping those in need without expecting anything in return.

9. "Oliver's Lost Toy"
Oliver loses his favorite toy, and his friends come together to help him find it. This story demonstrates empathy by understanding and acting upon someone else's distress.

10. "The Colorful Garden"
A garden where every flower is unique but valued equally teaches the lesson of empathy through diversity and inclusion.

Songs to Teach Empathy:

Here are 10 children's songs that are particularly effective in teaching empathy. These songs are crafted to be accessible and engaging for young minds, helping them understand and connect with the feelings of others:

1. **"Be Kind to Your Web-Footed Friends" – Traditional**: This fun and light-hearted song teaches children about being kind to everyone, regardless of their differences.
2. **"If You're Happy and You Know It" – Traditional**: This classic song can be adapted to explore different emotions, helping children understand and empathize with a range of feelings.
3. **"The Rainbow Song" – Kira Willey**: A song that celebrates diversity and understanding, encouraging children to appreciate and empathize with people's different experiences and backgrounds.
4. **"Don't Laugh at Me" – Peter, Paul, and Mary**: This song teaches children about the hurt that teasing can cause and the importance of accepting others.

5. **"How Kind" – MaryLee Sunseri**: A gentle song that encourages acts of kindness and helps children think about how their actions affect others.
6. **"Walk in Someone Else's Shoes" – Emily Arrow**: This song is about understanding and considering others' perspectives, an essential aspect of empathy.
7. **"What a Wonderful World" – Louis Armstrong (adapted for children)**: Though originally sung by Louis Armstrong, many child-friendly versions exist that teach kids to see and appreciate the beauty in the world and in other people.
8. **"Friend of Mine (I Wanna Grow Up)" – Catherine Feeny**: A song that speaks to the value of friendship and understanding, highlighting empathy in relationships.
9. **"Consideration" – Caspar Babypants**: This song is all about thinking of others and being considerate, which is a key part of being empathetic.
10. **"Kindness Begins with Me" – Teaching Tolerance**: A simple yet profound song that encourages children to start acts of kindness and empathy in their own lives. These songs can be a valuable part of an early childhood education curriculum, providing a musical and fun way to discuss and understand empathy. They can spark conversations, role-playing activities, and further exploration of emotions and how we relate to others.

Chapter III
Nurturing Kindness

Developing and Nurturing Kindness:

The Seedling Stage: Recognizing Emotions in Ourselves and Others

As we embark on the journey of nurturing kindness in young minds, it's essential to start with the foundations – recognizing and understanding emotions. Just like a gardener who understands the needs of each seedling, early childhood educators must help children identify and express their feelings. This chapter introduces engaging activities that aid children in recognizing a wide range of emotions, both in themselves and in others. Through story-telling, role-playing, and interactive games, we create a safe space where emotions are not just words, but lived experiences that children can relate to and understand.

Watering the Seeds: Empathy through Storytelling

Storytelling is a powerful tool in the empathy garden. It allows children to step into someone else's shoes, see the world from different perspectives, and develop empathy. This section provides a collection of age-appropriate stories that highlight themes of kindness, understanding, and respect. By discussing characters' feelings and actions, children learn to empathize with different situations. The guide includes questions and discussion points for each story, making it easier for educators to facilitate thoughtful conversations.

Pruning and Guidance: Role-Playing and Conflict Resolution

Role-playing activities are essential in teaching children how to navigate social situations and resolve conflicts with kindness. This part of the chapter offers a series of role-playing scenarios that mimic real-life situations children may encounter. From sharing toys to dealing with disagreements, these activities provide a practical framework for children to practice kindness and understanding. The guide emphasizes the importance of guidance and positive reinforcement from educators during these activities, ensuring that the lessons of empathy and kindness are deeply rooted.

The Blossoming of Kindness: Community Projects and Group Activities

The final section of this chapter focuses on bringing the lessons of empathy and kindness beyond the classroom. It suggests community projects and group activities that encourage children to apply their empathy skills in real-world settings. Whether it's a visit to a local nursing home or a classroom project to help a charity, these activities solidify the importance of kindness and empathy in everyday life. By participating in these projects, children not only practice kindness but also see its positive impact on others, reinforcing the value of empathy and understanding in building a caring community.

Acts of Kindness as Pathways to Empathy

Planting the Seeds of Kindness

In the Empathy Garden, every act of kindness is a seed that can grow into a beautiful display of empathy and understanding. This first part of Chapter 3 focuses on how simple, everyday acts of kindness can nurture a child's capacity for empathy. We begin by introducing the concept of kindness in tangible ways to young learners. Through stories, discussions, and hands-on activities, children learn that kindness is not just a feeling but a choice of action that can positively affect others and themselves.

Cultivating Empathy through Kind Actions

Empathy grows from understanding and sharing the feelings of others. By encouraging children to engage in acts of kindness, we help them to connect with the emotions and experiences of those around them. This section of the chapter provides a variety of activities that encourage children to perform kind deeds in their daily lives. From sharing toys and helping a friend, to writing thank-you notes and creating kindness crafts, these activities are designed to be fun, interactive, and meaningful.

Observing the Effects of Kindness

Fostering kindness in children involves guiding them to observe and comprehend the consequences of their actions. This chapter underscores the importance of reflective practices, encouraging children to engage in discussions and share the emotions generated by acts of kindness. Through this reflection, children develop a stronger awareness that their actions possess the power to create positive impacts on both themselves and others, nurturing a deeper sense of empathy.

Creating a Kindness Calendar

To reinforce the habit of kindness, the chapter introduces the concept of a Kindness Calendar. This tool serves as a daily reminder for children to engage in small acts of kindness. Each day presents a new opportunity for a kind act, whether it's helping a family member, smiling at a friend, or taking care of a pet. The calendar also includes spaces for children to record their acts of kindness and reflect on their feelings and the reactions of others.

Bringing Kindness into the Community

Lastly, the chapter encourages extending acts of kindness beyond the classroom and into the community. This section suggests organized group activities like visiting a local shelter to donate toys, making cards for healthcare workers, or planting a community garden. These activities not only cultivate empathy in children but also teach them about the power of collective kindness and its ability to foster a more compassionate and understanding community.

Interactive Activities that Encourage Kindness

Introduction

Building upon the foundation of understanding and practicing acts of kindness, Part 2 of Chapter 3 delves into interactive activities specifically designed to encourage kindness in young children. These activities are not only fun and engaging but also serve as practical tools for educators to instill empathy and kindness in their students.

1. Kindness Story Circle

Gather the children in a circle and read a story that focuses on kindness. After reading, discuss the kind actions in the story and how they made the characters feel. Encourage the children to share times when they were kind or someone was kind to them.

2. Compliment Jar

Create a compliment jar in the classroom. Encourage children to write or draw compliments for their classmates and place them in the jar. Regularly read these compliments out loud to foster a positive and supportive environment.

3. Helping Hands Chart

Create a chart with tasks that help others, like watering plants or organizing books. Each child can choose a task to complete each week, promoting responsibility and kindness through helping with communal tasks.

4. Role-Play Scenarios

Develop role-play scenarios that involve acts of kindness, such as sharing toys or helping a friend who is sad. These role-plays help children understand and practice empathy and kindness in a controlled, playful environment.

5. Kindness Postcards

Have the children create kindness postcards, drawing pictures and writing messages of kindness. These can be sent to family members, friends, or even local community helpers to spread kindness beyond the classroom.

6. The Kindness Tree

Create a kindness tree on a classroom wall. Each time a child performs a kind act, they can add a leaf to the tree. This visual representation of kindness growing can be incredibly motivating and rewarding for children.

7. Emotion Charades

Play a game of emotion charades, where children act out different feelings and others guess what they are. This activity helps children understand and empathize with a range of emotions, a key component of kindness.

8. Community Cleanup Day

Organize a community cleanup day where children can participate in cleaning up a local park or community area. This activity teaches children about caring for their environment and the importance of community service.

9. Friendship Bracelets

Guide the children in making friendship bracelets for each other. This activity not only fosters creativity but also encourages children to think about and appreciate their friends.

10. Thank You Notes to Community Workers

Have the children write thank you notes or create artwork to show appreciation for community workers like firefighters, nurses, or teachers. This activity helps children recognize and appreciate the kindness of others in their community.

Conclusion:

All these activities are crafted to suit different age groups and can seamlessly become part of daily or weekly routines. Through the consistent integration of these interactive activities, educators have the opportunity to establish a nurturing atmosphere. In this environment, kindness and empathy are not merely subjects taught; rather, they are experiences that are regularly practiced. This approach aims to cultivate a profound understanding and practical application of these essential social-emotional skills in young children.

Teaching kindness in early childhood is a vital aspect of social and emotional development. Here are some strategies and activities to incorporate kindness principles into early learning, along with a list of books and songs that can support these efforts.

Strategies and Activities

1. **Kindness Jar**: Create a jar where children can add a marble or a token every time they perform an act of kindness. Once the jar is full, celebrate with a class party or a special activity.
2. **Compliment Circle**: Have children sit in a circle and take turns giving compliments to the person next to them. This fosters a positive classroom environment and encourages children to notice good qualities in others.
3. **Role-Playing**: Engage children in role-playing activities where they act out scenarios that require kindness and empathy. Discuss the outcomes and feelings associated with each scenario.
4. **Kindness Tree**: Create a classroom kindness tree where children add a leaf every time they do something kind. This visual representation helps reinforce the concept of kindness.
5. **Storytelling**: Use storytelling sessions to narrate tales that focus on kindness and empathy. After the story, discuss the moral and how the characters showed kindness.
6. **Helping Hands**: Encourage children to help each other and adults in the classroom. Recognize these actions publicly to reinforce the behavior.
7. **Emotion Cards**: Use cards with different emotions to help children understand and empathize with various feelings. Discuss how kind actions can impact these emotions.
8. **Gratitude Journal**: Introduce a gratitude journal where children can draw or write about things they are thankful for, encouraging a positive and kind outlook.
9. **Kindness Calendar**: Create a monthly calendar with daily acts of kindness that children can perform. This could include things like sharing a toy, helping a friend, or saying something nice.
10. **Crafting for a Cause**: Engage children in crafting projects like making cards or gifts for people in need or community helpers, teaching them kindness through action.

Books on Kindness

1. "Have You Filled a Bucket Today?" by Carol McCloud
2. "Kindness is Cooler, Mrs. Ruler" by Margery Cuyler
3. "The Invisible Boy" by Trudy Ludwig
4. "Each Kindness" by Jacqueline Woodson
5. "The Lion and the Mouse" by Jerry Pinkney
6. "The Rainbow Fish" by Marcus Pfister
7. "Stick and Stone" by Beth Ferry
8. "A Sick Day for Amos McGee" by Philip C. Stead
9. "The Giving Tree" by Shel Silverstein
10. "We're All Wonders" by R.J. Palacio

Songs About Kindness

1. "Don't Laugh at Me" by Peter, Paul, and Mary
2. "It's Cool to Be Kind" by Nancy Kopman
3. "Be Kind to Your Web-Footed Friends" – Traditional
4. "Count on Me" by Bruno Mars
5. "What a Wonderful World" by Louis Armstrong
6. "Lean on Me" by Bill Withers
7. "Can't Stop the Feeling" by Justin Timberlake
8. "Rainbow Connection" by Kermit the Frog
9. "True Colors" by Cyndi Lauper
10. "You've Got a Friend in Me" by Randy Newman

Incorporating these strategies, activities, books, and songs into your teaching will create an enriching environment where young children can learn and practice kindness in meaningful ways.

Chapter IV
Understanding Emotions

Helping Educators Foster a Deeper Understanding of Emotions

The Landscape of Emotions

Emotions are like the weather in a garden: ever-changing, sometimes unpredictable, but always essential for growth. Just as a gardener needs to understand the climate to cultivate a thriving garden, educators must comprehend the emotional landscape of children to nurture their development. This section introduces the concept of basic emotions – happiness, sadness, anger, fear, surprise, and disgust – and explores how they manifest in young children. Interactive activities are suggested to help children recognize and name these emotions in themselves and others.

Cultivating Emotional Awareness

Here, we focus on developing emotional awareness in children. This involves teaching them to notice and describe their feelings. Activities like "Emotion Charades" and "Feeling Faces" are designed to make this learning process engaging and accessible. The section emphasizes the importance of validating all emotions, teaching children that it is okay to feel what they feel.

The Garden of Empathy

Empathy is the ability to understand and share the feelings of another. This section introduces practical tools and activities to cultivate empathy. Storytelling is a powerful method used here, where children are encouraged to step into the shoes of characters and explore their emotions. The section also covers how to create an "Empathy Corner" in the classroom, a safe space where children can express and discuss their feelings.

Emotional Regulation: Weeding Out the Overwhelm

Emotional regulation is key to maintaining a healthy emotional garden. This section provides strategies and activities to help children learn how to manage intense emotions. Techniques such as deep breathing, counting to ten, and using words to express feelings are explored. The chapter includes a guide for educators on how to model these techniques effectively.

Harvesting Emotional Intelligence

The concluding section of this chapter emphasizes the long-term benefits of emotional intelligence. It discusses how understanding and managing emotions contribute to success in school, relationships, and life. It also offers tips for educators to continue nurturing these skills beyond the classroom, ensuring that the seeds of empathy and understanding sown here continue to grow and flourish.

Teach Children to Recognize and Understand Different Emotions

Introduction to the World of Emotions

Welcome to the initial segment of Chapter 4 in "The Empathy Garden: Growing Kindness & Understanding in Young Minds." This portion is designed to assist educators in instructing children on the identification and comprehension of various emotions. Emotions serve as the vibrant hues that adorn our experiences, and grasping them holds paramount importance in the emotional and social development of young children.

Identifying Emotions: The First Steps

The journey begins with helping children identify different emotions. This section introduces simple yet engaging activities, such as using emotion cards with facial expressions or storytelling with emotive characters. These tools aid children in associating specific feelings with words and expressions. For instance, reading a story and pausing to ask, "How do you think the character feels now?" helps children connect emotions to situations.

Emotions Are Like Colors

In this part, emotions are compared to a palette of colors. Just as we mix colors to create art, emotions blend to shape our experiences. Activities like "Emotion Color Wheel" where children link emotions to colors (e.g., happy with yellow, sad with blue) are included. This visual and interactive approach makes the concept of emotions tangible and understandable for young minds.

The Language of Emotions

Language plays a pivotal role in understanding emotions. This section emphasizes the importance of teaching children emotional vocabulary. Simple games like "Emotion Word Bingo" can make learning new words fun. By expanding their emotional vocabulary, children can better express and understand their feelings and the feelings of others.

Facial Expressions and Body Language

Children are naturally observant. This section explores teaching children to notice and interpret facial expressions and body language as a way of understanding emotions. Activities like "Mimic and Guess" where children mimic an emotion and others guess, help develop this skill. Educators are provided with tips on how to guide children in understanding that the same emotion can be expressed differently by different people.

Understanding Emotions in Others

Empathy begins with understanding emotions in others. This part includes activities that encourage children to observe and discuss how characters in stories or peers in the classroom might be feeling. Role-playing scenarios are especially effective in this regard, as they allow children to step into someone else's shoes.

Concluding Thoughts

By the end of this section, educators will have a suite of tools and techniques to help children recognize and understand a range of emotions. The aim is to build a strong foundation for emotional intelligence, which will be further developed in subsequent chapters. The journey through 'The Empathy Garden' is not just about learning; it's about experiencing, understanding, and growing.

10 Activities for Identifying Emotions in Themselves and Others

1. **Emotion Matching Game**: Create cards with various emotions depicted through facial expressions. Children can play a matching game, pairing cards that display the same emotion. This activity helps in recognizing and naming different emotions.
2. **Feelings Circle Time**: Start each day with a feelings circle, where each child shares how they feel using words or an emotion chart. This encourages children to acknowledge their own emotions and understand the emotions of their peers.
3. **Story Time Emotion Exploration**: While reading a story, pause to ask questions like, "How do you think this character is feeling?" Encourage children to explain why they think the character feels that way, linking emotions to context.
4. **Emotion Charades**: Children act out an emotion without using words, while others guess the emotion. This activity helps in understanding body language and facial expressions associated with different feelings.
5. **Emotion Art**: Provide art materials for children to create artwork that expresses different emotions. This is a non-verbal way for children to explore and communicate feelings.
6. **Mood Meter Check-in**: Create a mood meter with different emotion zones. Throughout the day, children can move their personal marker to the zone that matches their current feelings. This activity aids in self-awareness of emotions.
7. **Role-Playing Scenarios**: Set up scenarios where children have to act out different emotions. This not only helps in identifying emotions but also in understanding the appropriate emotional response in various situations.

8. **Music and Emotions**: Play different types of music and discuss how each piece makes the children feel. This connects emotions with auditory experiences and teaches children how moods can be influenced by music.
9. **Photography of Emotions**: Show children various photographs portraying different emotions. Ask them to identify the emotions and discuss what might have caused these feelings in the people in the photos.
10. **Emotion Journaling**: Older preschoolers can keep a simple journal where they draw or write about their feelings and experiences. This practice encourages reflection and helps in recognizing patterns in emotional responses.

Conclusion:

These activities are crafted to be age-appropriate and engaging, making the exploration of emotions an interactive and insightful experience for young children. By participating in these activities, children not only learn to identify different emotions in themselves and others but also start developing empathy and emotional intelligence from a young age.

As an early childhood social-emotional educator, understanding and teaching emotions are fundamental to developing kindness and empathy in young children. Here are some strategies and activities that can be effectively used to teach young children about emotions and kindness, followed by a list of books and songs to reinforce these concepts.

Strategies and Activities for Understanding Emotions and Kindness

1. **Emotion Matching Game**: Create cards with different facial expressions or scenarios depicting various emotions. Children can match cards with similar emotions or identify what emotion is being displayed.
2. **Feelings Chart**: Use a chart with different emotions displayed. Children can use markers or stickers to indicate how they are feeling each day, promoting awareness and discussion about emotions.
3. **Story Time with Emotions**: Read stories and ask children to identify the emotions of the characters. Discuss why the characters might feel that way and how kindness could impact their feelings.
4. **Emotion Role-Play**: Have children act out different emotions and let others guess the emotion. This activity helps children understand and express emotions better.
5. **Crafting Emotion Masks**: Let children create masks that show different emotions. This activity can be followed by a discussion about what causes these emotions and how to respond to them.
6. **Kindness Brainstorming**: Have a group discussion to brainstorm ways to show kindness in response to various emotions. For example, what can we do when someone is sad or angry?
7. **Emotion Charades**: Play charades where children act out different emotions and others guess what they are. This encourages empathy by putting children in others' shoes.
8. **Emotion-Based Story Creation**: Children create their own stories focusing on characters' emotions and how they deal with them. This fosters creativity and emotional understanding.
9. **Yoga and Mindfulness**: Incorporate yoga and mindfulness activities that focus on understanding one's own emotions and cultivating calmness and kindness.
10. **Gratitude Circle**: Encourage children to share something or someone they are grateful for. This practice promotes positive emotions and a culture of appreciation and kindness.

Books on Emotions and Kindness

1. "The Color Monster: A Story About Emotions" by Anna Llenas
2. "In My Heart: A Book of Feelings" by Jo Witek
3. "The Way I Feel" by Janan Cain
4. "My Many Colored Days" by Dr. Seuss
5. "The Feelings Book" by Todd Parr
6. "Grumpy Bird" by Jeremy Tankard
7. "When Sophie Gets Angry - Really, Really Angry" by Molly Bang
8. "Glad Monster, Sad Monster" by Ed Emberley & Anne Miranda
9. "Today I Feel Silly & Other Moods That Make My Day" by Jamie Lee Curtis
10. "Feelings" by Aliki

Songs About Emotions and Kindness

1. "If You're Happy and You Know It" – Traditional
2. "Feelings" by Morris Albert
3. "Happy" by Pharrell Williams
4. "Skidamarlnk" – Traditional
5. "I've Got So Much to Give" by Barry White
6. "Smile" by Uncle Kracker
7. "Shake It Off" by Taylor Swift
8. "Let It Go" from Disney's Frozen
9. "The Bear Went Over the Mountain" – Traditional
10. "Beautiful Day" by U2

Integrating these strategies, activities, books, and songs into your curriculum will help young children better understand and express their emotions, and develop kindness and empathy towards others.

Chapter V
The Empathy Garden Grows

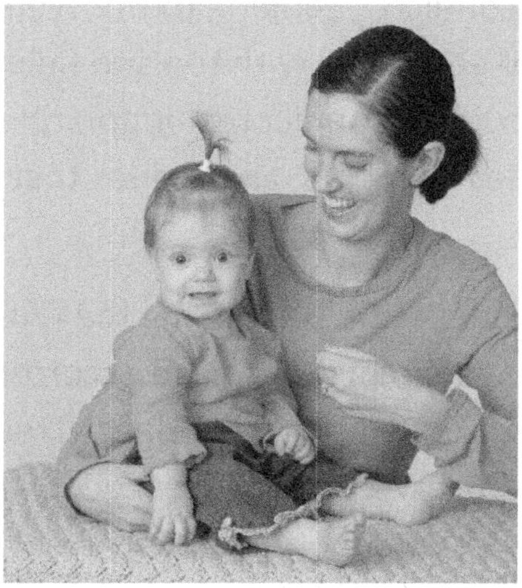

The Heart of the Empathy Garden

In the heart of our journey through "The Empathy Garden," we arrive at a pivotal stage where understanding and kindness, like young seedlings, begin to take root deeply in the fertile soil of young minds. Chapter 5, "The Empathy Garden Grows," is designed to nurture these seedlings into blossoming, empathetic behaviors.

As we step into this chapter, imagine a garden rich with the vibrant colors of empathy and compassion. Here, each child is both a gardener and a part of the garden, learning to cultivate their understanding of others' feelings and perspectives. We start by introducing the concept of 'emotional soil' – a metaphor for the nurturing environment needed for empathy to grow. This includes trust, safety, and openness, elements that are as crucial to empathy as sunlight and water are to a garden.

Next, we delve into 'Planting Seeds of Kindness.' This section focuses on practical activities that children can engage in to develop empathy. Simple, yet powerful exercises like role-playing, sharing stories about feelings, and group discussions about diverse perspectives help children understand and respect the feelings of others. These activities are not just about talking; they involve active listening, a key skill in developing empathy.

As our empathy garden grows, we address the inevitable challenges. Just as gardens face pests and weeds, children encounter obstacles like misunderstandings and conflicts. 'Tending to the Weeds' is a crucial part of this chapter, where we equip educators with tools to help children navigate these challenges. Techniques such as conflict resolution role-play, guided discussions about feelings during disagreements, and stories that illustrate peaceful problem-solving are included.

The chapter concludes with 'Harvesting the Fruits of Empathy.' This section celebrates the growth and learning that have occurred. It includes ideas for empathy-based projects, like creating a 'Kindness Tree' where children can display acts of kindness they've observed or experienced, or a 'Feeling Flowerbed' where each petal represents different emotions they've learned to recognize and respect in others and themselves.

"The Empathy Garden Grows" is a chapter filled with hope and practical strategies. It is an invitation to educators to cultivate a generation of children who not only understand their own emotions but are also adept at recognizing and respecting the emotions of others. Through this empathetic approach, we lay the foundation for a more compassionate and understanding world.

Cultivating Friendships through Empathy

As we begin Chapter 5 of "The Empathy Garden: Growing Kindness & Understanding in Young Minds," we focus on the vital role empathy plays in fostering friendships and positive interactions among young children. This chapter, titled "Cultivating Friendships through Empathy," explores how empathy, the ability to understand and share the feelings of others, is a foundational block in building strong, healthy relationships.

The journey starts with the concept of empathy as a seed – a small yet potent beginning. We explain to the children how this 'seed of empathy' when planted, can grow into beautiful connections with those around them. We introduce stories and activities designed to help children recognize emotions in themselves and others, a crucial step in developing empathy. Activities like 'Emotion Charades' or 'Feelings Circle' where children express and guess emotions, help them understand that everyone experiences a range of feelings.

Next, we guide the children to see how empathy leads to kind actions. Through role-playing and group discussions, we demonstrate how understanding someone else's feelings can lead to compassionate responses. For instance, when a friend is sad, understanding their feelings might lead to comforting them or offering help. This section of the chapter emphasizes how empathetic actions are the roots that strengthen friendships.

The chapter also explores the concept of 'empathy in action' in the playground or classroom. We encourage children to notice and respond to the feelings of their peers. Simple gestures like sharing a toy, inviting someone to play, or just listening to a classmate, are highlighted as examples of empathy in action. These actions not only build friendships but also create a positive, inclusive atmosphere in the group.

In this part of the chapter, we also address the challenges children might face in understanding and relating to others. We provide educators with tools to help children navigate these situations, emphasizing that misunderstandings are opportunities for learning and growth in empathy.

As the chapter concludes, we reflect on the beautiful 'garden of friendships' that empathy helps to cultivate. Children learn that, just like in a garden, diversity in friendships – understanding and appreciating differences in others – adds to the beauty and richness of their experiences. This section includes activities like creating a 'Friendship Flowerbed,' where each flower represents a friend and their unique qualities, reinforcing the idea that empathy is at the heart of every meaningful friendship.

Stories and Activities to Cultivate Empathic Behaviors

In the second part of Chapter 5

, "The Empathy Garden Grows," we delve into the importance of integrating stories and activities into the curriculum to highlight empathetic behaviors in various situations. This section is designed to offer educators a toolkit for nurturing empathy in young minds through engaging and relatable content.

The Power of Stories in Teaching Empathy

Stories are a powerful medium for teaching empathy. They allow children to step into the shoes of others and experience different perspectives and emotions. This part of the chapter introduces ten carefully selected stories, each illustrating empathy in different contexts:

1. **"The Rainbow Fish"** by Marcus Pfister: Teaches the value of sharing and the joy it brings.
2. **"Stand in My Shoes"** by Bob Sornson: Highlights understanding others' feelings.
3. **"Chrysanthemum"** by Kevin Henkes: Addresses empathy in the context of teasing and acceptance.
4. **"A Chair for My Mother"** by Vera B. Williams: Showcases empathy and support in family settings.
5. **"The Invisible Boy"** by Trudy Ludwig: Focuses on inclusion and noticing those who feel left out.
6. **"Last Stop on Market Street"** by Matt de la Peña: Encourages understanding of diverse lifestyles and gratitude.
7. **"The Name Jar"** by Yangsook Choi: Deals with cultural understanding and acceptance.
8. **"Enemy Pie"** by Derek Munson: Teaches about resolving conflicts and making friends.
9. **"My Friend is Sad"** by Mo Willems: Illustrates how to recognize and respond to friends' emotions.
10. **"The Smallest Girl in the Smallest Grade"** by Justin Roberts: Empowers children to make a difference, no matter their size.

Activities to Reinforce Empathetic Behaviors

Complementing these stories, the chapter offers ten activities that reinforce empathetic behaviors. These activities are designed to be interactive, fun, and reflective, allowing children to practice empathy in various scenarios:

1. **Emotion Matching Game**: Children match facial expressions to corresponding emotions.
2. **Role-Play Scenarios**: Acting out different situations to understand others' perspectives.
3. **Empathy Art**: Creating artwork that expresses feelings or depicts scenes of kindness.
4. **'Walk in Their Shoes' Relay**: A relay race where children walk in oversized shoes, symbolizing understanding others' experiences.
5. **Feelings Journal**: Encouraging children to write or draw about different emotions they observe or experience.
6. **Kindness Role-Playing**: Children act out scenes of helping and supporting others.
7. **'What Would You Do?'**: Discussion-based activity where children suggest empathetic responses to various scenarios.
8. **'Compliment Flower' Craft**: Each petal has a written compliment for a classmate, teaching appreciation.
9. **Empathy Bingo**: A game where children identify empathetic actions like listening or helping.
10. **'The Emotion Wheel'**: A tool to help children identify and express their emotions more accurately.

By combining the rich, emotional narratives of these stories with the practical application of the activities, aims to deeply embed empathetic understanding and behaviors in young children. This combination of storytelling and experiential learning forms a comprehensive approach, equipping children with the emotional tools they need to navigate their world with kindness and understanding.

Chapter VI
Weathering the Storms

The Empathy Garden: Growing Kindness & Understanding

In Chapter 6, "Weathering the Storms," we explore the vital aspect of resilience and emotional strength in young children. Just like a garden facing unexpected weather, our young learners will encounter various emotional storms throughout their growth. This chapter aims to equip early childhood educators with tools and strategies to nurture resilience and empathy, enabling children to thrive amidst life's challenges.

The Power of Understanding Emotions: The journey begins by helping children recognize and understand their emotions. Through engaging activities and story-telling, we teach them to identify feelings like happiness, sadness, anger, and fear. This emotional literacy lays the foundation for empathy, as children start to understand that others experience similar emotions.

Creating a Safe Emotional Space: Children need a safe environment to express their emotions without fear or judgment. We discuss how to create such spaces in classrooms, using tools like 'emotion corners' or 'feelings charts'. These spaces encourage open communication, making it easier for children to share their feelings and experiences.

Empathy Through Role-Playing: Role-playing exercises are a powerful tool in teaching empathy. By acting out different scenarios, children learn to put themselves in others' shoes, understanding how their actions affect others. This chapter provides practical role-playing activities designed to foster empathy and kindness.

Resilience Through Storytelling: Stories have a unique way of conveying lessons on resilience and coping. This section offers a curated list of children's books that teach about overcoming difficulties, adapting to change, and the strength found in kindness and helping others.

Nurturing Emotional Intelligence: Emotional intelligence is key to weathering emotional storms. We cover techniques to help children manage their emotions effectively, such as deep breathing, mindfulness, and positive self-talk. These skills are not only crucial for emotional regulation but also for building strong relationships.

Empathy in Action - Community Projects: Finally, we propose community projects that allow children to practice empathy in real-world settings. These projects, such as visiting a local nursing home or organizing a charity drive, give children a sense of purpose and belonging, reinforcing the values of kindness and understanding.

Addressing Challenges to Empathy Such as Conflict or Misunderstanding

In the first part of Chapter 6, "Weathering the Storms," we delve into the challenges to empathy in early childhood, focusing on conflict and misunderstanding. These challenges, like harsh weather in a garden, can hinder the growth of empathy if not addressed thoughtfully. Our aim in this section is to provide educators with insights and strategies to navigate these challenges effectively.

Understanding the Roots of Conflict: Conflict is a natural part of human interaction, and it is no different for young children. It often stems from a lack of understanding, communication issues, or differing needs and wants. We begin by exploring the common causes of conflicts among young children and how these can impede the development of empathy.

Empathy in the Face of Conflict: Teaching children to maintain empathy during conflicts is crucial. This section discusses strategies to help children understand the perspective of others, even when they are in disagreement. Techniques such as active listening, expressing feelings using "I" statements, and learning to recognize non-verbal cues are elaborated upon.

The Role of Misunderstandings in Empathy Development: Misunderstandings are frequent in early childhood due to developing language and social skills. In this section, we explore how these misunderstandings can lead to hurt feelings or conflict and how educators can turn these moments into valuable empathy-building opportunities.

Navigating Misunderstandings through Empathy Building Exercises: This part provides practical exercises designed to help children understand and respect differing viewpoints. Activities may include group problem-solving tasks, storytelling with different perspectives, and games that encourage perspective-taking.

Fostering a Culture of Open Communication: Creating an environment where children feel safe to express their thoughts and feelings is essential for empathy to flourish. Techniques to foster open communication in the classroom are discussed, emphasizing the importance of a non-judgmental, supportive approach.

Empathy, Conflict Resolution, and Peer Relationships: Lastly, we address how developing empathy skills can aid in conflict resolution and lead to stronger, more compassionate peer relationships. This section includes guided activities that promote cooperation, understanding, and kindness among young learners.

Strategies for Maintaining Empathy in Difficult Situations

"Weathering the Storms," we turn our focus to the strategies for maintaining empathy in difficult situations. Children, much like delicate plants in a garden, require nurturing to stay resilient and empathetic during challenging times. This section outlines ten practical strategies that early childhood educators can use to help children maintain empathy, even in the face of adversity.

1. **Modeling Empathetic Behavior**: Children learn by example. Show empathy in your interactions with them and others. This modeling teaches them how to be empathetic in their own relationships.
2. **Encouraging Expression of Feelings**: Create a classroom environment where children feel comfortable expressing their emotions. Use activities such as drawing or storytelling to allow them to communicate their feelings.
3. **Active Listening Exercises**: Teach children the skill of active listening. Use role-play and group activities to practice listening to others without interruption and reflecting back what they have heard.
4. **Empathy Role-Playing**: Engage children in role-playing exercises where they take on different roles and perspectives. This helps them understand and empathize with different viewpoints.
5. **Emotion Recognition Activities**: Use games and activities to help children recognize and understand different emotions, both in themselves and others. This can include facial expression matching games or emotion charades.
6. **Mindfulness Practices**: Introduce simple mindfulness exercises that help children become more aware of their own feelings and the feelings of others. This can include breathing exercises or guided meditations focused on empathy.
7. **Developing a Vocabulary for Emotions**: Help children develop a rich vocabulary for expressing emotions. Use discussions, books, and activities to introduce new emotion words and concepts.
8. **Conflict Resolution Role-Playing**: Use role-playing scenarios to teach children effective conflict resolution skills. Focus on finding win-win solutions and understanding the other person's perspective.
9. **Empathy Circle Discussions**: Regularly hold group discussions where children can share experiences and listen to others. This 'empathy circle' can be a safe space for discussing feelings and learning from each other.
10. **Community Service Projects**: Involve children in community service projects that require them to think about and help others. This could include making cards for people in hospitals or helping in a community garden.

Chapter VII
Harvesting the Rewards

The Benefits of Empathy for the Individual or Community

In the sixth chapter of "The Empathy Garden: Growing Kindness & Understanding in Young Minds," we delve into the profound benefits that empathy brings to both individuals and the community. Empathy, often nurtured in the early stages of development, has far-reaching impacts that extend beyond the classroom. Here, we discuss ten key benefits that highlight the importance of empathy in shaping well-rounded, compassionate individuals and a supportive community.

1. **Improved Communication Skills:** Empathetic children learn to listen actively and understand others' perspectives. This skill is crucial for effective communication, enabling them to express themselves clearly and understand others better.

2. **Enhanced Emotional Intelligence:** The role of empathy in emotional intelligence is substantial. Children who possess empathy demonstrate enhanced abilities in recognizing and regulating their own emotions, as well as comprehending the emotions of others. This heightened awareness forms a fundamental foundation for both personal and social success.

3. **Stronger Relationships:** Empathy fosters deeper connections. Children who show empathy are more likely to develop strong, healthy relationships with their peers, family members, and educators, as they can relate to and understand others' feelings.

4. **Reduced Bullying Incidences:** Empathy in children leads to a decrease in bullying behaviors. By understanding and appreciating the feelings of others, children are less likely to engage in actions that harm their peers.
5. **Enhanced Conflict Resolution Skills:** Empathetic children are better equipped to resolve conflicts amicably. They can view situations from multiple perspectives and find solutions that are considerate of everyone involved.
6. **Increased Tolerance and Acceptance:** Empathy encourages tolerance and acceptance of differences. It teaches children to appreciate diversity and fosters an inclusive environment where every individual is respected and valued.
7. **Better Academic Performance:** Studies have shown that empathy is linked to better academic performance. Empathetic children often have a greater capacity for teamwork and adaptability, skills that are beneficial in educational settings.
8. **Heightened Self-Esteem:** Empathy helps in building self-esteem. Children who are empathetic take pride in their ability to understand and support others, which in turn boosts their own sense of self-worth.
9. **Community Cohesion:** On a broader scale, empathy contributes to community cohesion. When children carry empathetic values into adulthood, they help create a more compassionate, understanding society.
10. **Promotion of Leadership Qualities:** Empathy is a key trait in effective leaders. It enables individuals to connect with others, inspire, and lead with compassion and understanding.

In conclusion, empathy is more than just an admirable trait, but a foundational skill that offers a multitude of benefits. It shapes children into understanding, compassionate individuals and paves the way for a more empathetic, cohesive community. As we continue to cultivate this invaluable skill in our Empathy Garden, we not only enrich the lives of our young learners but also contribute to a kinder, more understanding world.

Real-Life Stories of How Empathy Made a Significant Difference

Now we turn our attention to real-life stories where empathy has made a significant and tangible difference. These stories, drawn from various contexts, illustrate the powerful impact empathy can have on individuals and communities. Here are ten such stories:

1. **The Classroom Conflict Resolved:** In a primary school, a conflict arose over a shared toy. Instead of escalating into a fight, one child empathized with her classmate's desire to play with the toy and suggested they play together. This simple act of understanding transformed a potential conflict into an opportunity for cooperative play.
2. **The Bully's Transformation:** A young boy known for bullying behavior experienced a change after his teacher helped him understand the emotions of those he bullied. This led to a complete transformation, with the boy becoming a champion for anti-bullying in his school.
3. **The Comforting Friend:** After a classmate lost a pet, a young girl showed extraordinary empathy by sharing her own experience of loss. Her understanding and comforting words helped her classmate cope with grief, showcasing the healing power of empathy.
4. **The Inclusive Playground Game:** A group of children included a child with physical disabilities in their playground game, modifying the rules so everyone could participate. This act of empathy created a sense of belonging and joy for all involved.
5. **The Empathy Project:** A school started an "empathy project," where children shared stories about times they felt sad or left out. This project fostered a culture of understanding and significantly reduced incidents of exclusion and bullying.
6. **The Young Environmentalist:** Moved by the plight of animals affected by pollution, a young student started a local cleanup initiative. His empathetic action not only helped the environment but also inspired his community to join in.
7. **The Kindergarten Helper:** A young child noticed a classmate struggling to tie their shoes. Remembering her own struggle, she offered to help, demonstrating empathy through her actions and words.

8. **The Supportive Sibling:** A child, whose sibling was diagnosed with autism, showed remarkable empathy by learning about the condition and helping their sibling navigate social situations, significantly improving their sibling's school experience.
9. **The Lunchtime Companion:** Noticing a new student eating alone, a group of students invited him to join their table. This small act of empathy helped the new student feel welcomed and quickly make friends.
10. **The Empathetic Listener:** A teacher noticed a student who seemed withdrawn and took the time to listen to her concerns. This empathetic approach revealed the student was dealing with family issues, leading to the provision of much-needed support.

Each of these stories highlights the profound transformative power of empathy. They stand as inspiring examples showcasing how empathy has the ability to bridge divides, mend emotional wounds, and contribute to the creation of a more compassionate and inclusive world. For educators and caregivers, these narratives serve as poignant reminders of the significant impact our endeavors in fostering empathy can make, extending beyond our classrooms and reaching into the broader world.

Skill Building Using the Emotional Skills Framework

Creating a nurturing environment is pivotal for the flourishing of empathy, and the Emotions Skills. Blossom serves as an excellent framework for cultivating emotional intelligence in young children. The integration of ten essential emotional skills — being loving, being grateful, being gentle, being respectful, being polite, being kind, being honest, being giving, being friendly, and being sympathetic — lays the foundation for well-rounded emotional development.

1. **Being Loving:** Encourage children to express love and affection through activities such as creating handmade cards for family members or engaging in role-playing scenarios that involve expressing love and care.
2. **Being Grateful:** Instill the habit of gratitude through daily practices, like keeping a gratitude journal or sharing something they are thankful for during group discussions.
3. **Being Gentle:** Teach gentleness through activities like reading books that emphasize gentle behavior, modeling gentle interactions with peers and animals, and incorporating soft, tactile materials into play.

4. **Being Respectful:** Promote respect by engaging in activities that emphasize the importance of listening, taking turns, and appreciating each other's opinions during group discussions or collaborative projects.
5. **Being Polite:** Integrate politeness into daily routines by teaching phrases like "please" and "thank you." Role-playing scenarios where children practice polite communication can be both fun and educational.
6. **Being Kind:** Promote acts of kindness through activities such as creating a kindness jar where children deposit notes about kind actions they witness or experience, fostering a culture of compassion.
7. **Being Honest:** Encourage honesty by reading stories that emphasize the value of truthfulness and engaging in discussions about the consequences of dishonesty.
8. **Being Giving:** Foster a giving spirit by organizing donation drives for local charities, sharing toys or books with peers, and engaging in activities that emphasize the joy of giving.
9. **Being Friendly:** Promote friendliness by organizing group games that encourage teamwork and collaboration, creating an atmosphere where children learn the importance of building positive relationships.
10. **Being Sympathetic:** Develop sympathy by incorporating activities that explore different perspectives, such as storytelling or role-playing scenarios that help children understand and empathize with others' feelings. The Emotions Skills Blossom, intertwined with these activities, provides a comprehensive approach to instilling essential emotional skills in young children, laying the groundwork for a future where empathy and compassion thrive.

Skill Building Using the Social Skills Framework

Nurturing empathy in young children is intrinsically linked to fostering a supportive environment, and the Social Skills Framework offers a valuable structure for developing emotional intelligence. Within this framework, ten essential emotional skills — being obedient, sharing, being happy, being cooperative, being a self-starter, being responsible, being helpful, being determined, being forgiving, and mastering self-control — serve as building blocks for well-rounded social and emotional development.

1. **Being Obedient:** Introduce the concept of obedience through interactive games that involve following instructions, reinforcing the importance of listening and respecting authority figures.

2. **Sharing:** Promote sharing by incorporating activities where children collaborate on projects, share toys during playtime, or take turns using shared resources, instilling the value of generosity.
3. **Being Happy:** Cultivate a positive mindset through activities that focus on gratitude, mindfulness, and the celebration of achievements, fostering an environment where happiness is acknowledged and shared.
4. **Being Cooperative:** Encourage cooperation through team-based activities, group projects, and cooperative games that emphasize the significance of working together toward common goals.
5. **Being a Self-Starter:** Foster independence and initiative by providing opportunities for children to take on leadership roles, make choices, and initiate activities within a structured environment.
6. **Being Responsible:** Teach responsibility through activities that involve taking care of personal belongings, completing assigned tasks, and understanding the consequences of one's actions.
7. **Being Helpful:** Promote a sense of helpfulness by encouraging children to assist their peers, teachers, or family members in various tasks, fostering a culture of mutual support.
8. **Being Determined:** Cultivate determination through goal-setting activities, where children learn the value of perseverance and hard work in achieving their objectives.
9. **Being Forgiving:** Introduce forgiveness through storytelling or role-playing scenarios that explore the concept of understanding, empathy, and letting go of negative feelings.
10. **Mastering Self-Control:** Develop self-control through mindfulness exercises, breathing techniques, and activities that encourage children to manage their emotions and impulses effectively. The integration of the Social Skills Framework into these activities provides a comprehensive approach to nurturing emotional skills in young children.

By emphasizing obedience, sharing, happiness, cooperation, self-starting behaviors, responsibility, helpfulness, determination, forgiveness, and self-control, educators and caregivers can contribute to a supportive environment where empathy can flourish, fostering a generation of socially adept and emotionally intelligent individuals.

Chapter VIII
The Ever-Blooming Garden

Nurturing Empathy Continuously

As we venture into the seventh chapter of "The Empathy Garden: Growing Kindness & Understanding in Young Minds," it becomes vital to emphasize the ongoing journey of nurturing empathy. The metaphor of an ever-blooming garden aptly represents the continuous nature of this development. Just as a garden requires consistent care and attention to flourish, so too does the cultivation of empathy in young minds.

Empathy, much like the plants in our garden, grows and evolves over time. It is not a one-time lesson, but a lifelong learning process that must be nurtured continuously. Young children, with their naturally curious and open hearts, are particularly receptive to learning about empathy. However, it is a skill that needs to be reinforced through practice, patience, and persistence.

In this chapter, we focus on practical strategies and activities that educators and parents can employ to foster an ongoing empathetic environment. Key to this is creating a safe space where children feel heard and valued. Listening to their thoughts and feelings without judgment encourages them to express themselves and, in turn, listen to others. This mutual understanding is the cornerstone of empathy.

Moreover, we explore the importance of role-modeling empathetic behavior. Children learn a great deal by observing the actions of adults around them. When educators and parents demonstrate empathy in their interactions, children absorb these behaviors and mirror them in their own relationships. Simple acts like acknowledging feelings, showing kindness in difficult situations, and being present in the moment are powerful lessons in empathy.

We also delve into the significance of storytelling and role-playing in developing empathy. Stories with diverse characters and situations expose children to different perspectives and life experiences, broadening their understanding and acceptance of others. Role-playing, on the other hand, allows children to step into someone else's shoes, fostering a deeper understanding of different emotions and viewpoints.

To ensure the empathy garden keeps blooming, regular reflection is crucial. Encourage children to reflect on their actions and feelings, and discuss how their behavior impacts others. This reflection helps to internalize empathetic responses and makes them more natural over time.

Lastly, we emphasize the importance of celebrating empathy in action. Recognizing and praising empathetic behavior reinforces its value and encourages its continuation. Whether it's sharing toys, helping a friend in distress, or simply being a good listener, every act of empathy is a vital bloom in the ever-growing garden of understanding and kindness.

In conclusion, cultivating empathy is an ongoing process that requires commitment, understanding, and patience. By consistently nurturing these qualities in young children, we lay the foundation for a more compassionate and empathetic world. The empathy garden, with its ever-blooming flowers, stands as a testament to the enduring power of kindness and understanding in shaping young minds.

10 Practical Strategies for Teaching Empathy

In Chapter 8 of "The Empathy Garden: Growing Kindness & Understanding in Young Minds," we focus on concrete strategies to teach and reinforce empathy in early childhood. These practices are designed to be both engaging and educational, helping children to understand and internalize empathetic behaviors.

1. **Emotion Matching Games**: Create games where children match facial expressions or scenarios with corresponding emotions. This helps them recognize and understand different feelings in themselves and others.

2. **Storytelling with Perspective-Taking**: Use storybooks or storytelling sessions to explore characters' feelings and motivations. Ask questions like, "How do you think [character] feels right now?" or "What would you do in their place?" This encourages children to put themselves in others' shoes.

3. **Empathy Circles**: Create a circle time where each child shares something about their day or how they're feeling. Encourage active listening, where children learn to listen without interrupting and then respond or ask questions about what was shared.

4. **Role-Playing Activities**: Engage children in role-play activities where they act out different scenarios. This not only helps them understand different perspectives but also teaches them appropriate ways to respond to others' emotions.

5. **Emotion Charades**: Similar to traditional charades, in this game, children act out different emotions and others guess what they are. This is a fun way to help children become more aware of how emotions can be expressed through body language and facial expressions.

6. **Empathy Reflection Journal**: Introduce a journal where children can draw or write about times when they felt a strong emotion or noticed someone else feeling an emotion. This practice encourages reflection and thoughtfulness about emotional experiences.

7. **Community Service Projects**: Involve children in simple community service projects, like making cards for people in hospitals or helping out in a community garden. These activities can foster a sense of empathy towards the broader community.

8. **Mindfulness and Emotional Regulation Exercises**: Teach children basic mindfulness techniques to help them understand and manage their emotions. This self-awareness is a key component of empathy.
9. **'Walk in Their Shoes' Discussions**: Have discussions about people from different backgrounds, cultures, or life situations. Use stories or videos to make these more relatable. Discuss how life might feel from their perspective, fostering a sense of global empathy.
10. **Empathy Praise and Recognition**: When a child demonstrates empathy, praise this behavior specifically. For example, "I saw how you comforted your friend when they were upset, that was very empathetic." This positive reinforcement makes children more likely to repeat empathetic behavior.

By integrating these strategies into the curriculum and daily interactions, educators and parents can provide children with a variety of opportunities to learn about and practice empathy.

Chapter IX
Activities and Resources for Educators and Parents

Chapter 9 of "The Empathy Garden: Growing Kindness & Understanding in Young Minds" emphasizes the critical importance of providing activities and resources to reinforce empathy learning for parents and educators. This chapter serves as a guide to understanding why these tools are essential in nurturing empathy and social-emotional skills in early childhood.

The Importance of Reinforcing Empathy Learning

Building a Foundation for Empathy

Empathy is not an innate skill; it is developed and nurtured over time. Early childhood is a crucial period for this development. By providing structured activities and resources, we can lay a strong foundation for empathy in young minds. These tools help children understand and recognize emotions, both in themselves and others, fostering a deep sense of empathy from a young age.

Enhancing Emotional Literacy

Activities and resources designed for empathy education play a significant role in enhancing emotional literacy among children. By engaging in these activities, children learn to identify, express, and manage their emotions effectively. This emotional literacy is a key component of empathy, as it enables children to relate to the feelings of others and respond appropriately.

Creating a Supportive Environment

The nurturing of empathy requires a supportive environment, and resources and activities play a crucial role in enabling parents and educators to establish such a setting. These resources offer practical ways to showcase empathy, kindness, and understanding, serving as a model for children to emulate. Furthermore, they equip adults with the tools necessary to address and resolve conflicts in a manner that underscores empathy and respect.

Promoting Inclusivity and Understanding

Empathy is closely tied to inclusivity and understanding of diversity. Activities that focus on empathy education encourage children to appreciate and respect differences. This understanding is vital in a globalized world where children will interact with diverse cultures, beliefs, and perspectives. Empathy-building activities help in nurturing open-minded and tolerant individuals.

Strengthening Parent-Child and Teacher-Student Bonds

Activities and resources for empathy education also serve to strengthen the bonds between parents and children, as well as between teachers and students. Engaging in these activities together builds trust and understanding, creating a deeper connection. This strong bond is essential for children to feel secure and valued, which in turn promotes social-emotional health.

Long-Term Benefits

The long-term benefits of empathy education cannot be overstated. Empathetic children grow into adults who can form healthy relationships, communicate effectively, and contribute positively to society. By investing in empathy-building activities and resources, we are investing in a more compassionate and understanding future generation.

In conclusion, Chapter 9 of "The Empathy Garden" highlights the indispensable role of activities and resources in empathy education. These tools are not just for immediate learning but are investments in the emotional and social well-being of children, shaping them into empathetic, understanding, and kind individuals. As educators and parents, utilizing these resources effectively is one of the most significant contributions we can make to a child's holistic development.

Practical Activities and Resource for Practicing Empathy

1. **Emotion Matching Game:** Create cards with different facial expressions representing emotions. Encourage children to match expressions with emotion names, fostering emotional literacy.
2. **Storytelling with Emotion:** Read stories and pause to ask children how characters might be feeling, encouraging them to put themselves in others' shoes.
3. **Role-Playing Scenarios:** Use role-play to act out various scenarios, helping children understand different perspectives and feelings.
4. **Empathy Circle:** Hold regular discussions where children share something about their day and others practice listening and showing empathy.
5. **Kindness Tree:** Create a tree on a bulletin board. Each time a child performs a kind act, add a leaf with their name on it, promoting positive behavior.
6. **Feelings Journal:** Encourage children to draw or write about their feelings in a personal journal, helping them understand and express emotions.
7. **Emotion Charades:** Play charades using emotion cards, enhancing children's ability to recognize and empathize with different feelings.
8. **Compliment Circle:** Sit in a circle and have each child give a compliment to the person next to them, building a culture of kindness.
9. **Helping Hands:** Involve children in simple acts of helping others, teaching the value of kindness and empathy in action.
10. **Gratitude Sharing:** End each day by sharing things each child is thankful for, fostering a sense of gratitude and empathy towards others.

Resources for Parents and Educators

1. **Books:** Curate a list of children's books that focus on empathy, kindness, and diversity.
2. **Websites:** Provide a list of websites with free resources, articles, and activities focused on teaching empathy to young children.
3. **Workshops:** Organize or suggest workshops for parents and educators on early childhood empathy development.

4. **Community Projects:** Encourage participation in community service projects suitable for young children.
5. **Podcasts and Videos:** Share educational and entertaining podcasts and videos that teach empathy and kindness.
6. **Professional Development:** Offer information on courses and seminars for educators to deepen their understanding of social-emotional learning.
7. **Parenting Forums:** Create or suggest online forums where parents can share experiences and advice on nurturing empathy in children.
8. **Educational Toys:** Recommend toys and games that promote cooperative play and understanding of emotions.
9. **Activity Guides:** Provide detailed guides for empathy-building activities that can be done at home or in the classroom.
10. **Support Groups:** Establish or recommend support groups for parents and educators to discuss challenges and successes in teaching empathy.

By integrating these activities and utilizing these resources, parents and educators can create a nurturing environment that encourages empathy, kindness, and understanding in young minds. This chapter aims to be a practical, hands-on guide to making 'The Empathy Garden' a reality in the lives of young children

Guided Discussions, Crafts, and Role-Playing Scenarios

1. **Feelings of the Day:** Start or end the day by discussing what made each child feel happy, sad, or angry, and why.
2. **Story Reflections:** After reading a story, discuss the feelings and actions of the characters and what children might do in similar situations.
3. **Community Helpers:** Talk about various community helpers and how they help others, emphasizing empathy and kindness.
4. **Friendship Talk:** Discuss what makes a good friend and how to be kind and understanding in friendships.
5. **Problem-Solving Discussions:** Present a simple problem and discuss various empathetic ways to solve it.

6. **Nature and Empathy:** Discuss how we should treat animals and plants, relating it to empathy for all living things.
7. **Cultural Appreciation:** Have discussions about different cultures and traditions to foster understanding and respect.
8. **Emotion Exploration:** Use pictures of different emotions and discuss what causes these feelings and how to respond.
9. **Acts of Kindness:** Share stories of kindness and discuss how small acts can make a big difference.
10. **Gratitude Moments:** Discuss what each child is grateful for and how expressing gratitude affects others and themselves.

Craft Ideas

1. **Emotion Masks:** Create masks showing different emotions to help children understand and express feelings.
2. **Kindness Rocks:** Paint rocks with kind messages or symbols and place them in community areas.
3. **Empathy Puppets:** Make puppets to use in role-playing various emotional scenarios.
4. **Thank You Cards:** Craft thank you cards for community helpers or family members.
5. **Friendship Bracelets:** Make bracelets to give to friends as a symbol of kindness and connection.
6. **World Culture Collage:** Create a collage using images representing various cultures to celebrate diversity.
7. **Emotion Wheel:** Make a wheel that displays different emotions to spin and discuss.
8. **Helping Hands Tree:** Create a tree where each handprint represents a kind deed.
9. **Feelings Booklet:** Each child creates a booklet illustrating different feelings and what causes them.
10. **Empathy Flowers:** Craft flowers with petals that list ways to show empathy and kindness.

Role-Playing Scenarios

1. **Helping a New Student:** Role-play how to welcome and help a new student in class.
2. **Sharing Toys:** Act out scenarios where children practice sharing and resolving conflicts over toys.
3. **Injured Friend:** Role-play helping a friend who has fallen and is hurt.
4. **Feeling Left Out:** Act out situations where a child feels left out and how to include them.
5. **Different Opinions:** Role-play a scenario where children have different opinions and learn to respect each other.
6. **Lost Pet:** Pretend a pet is lost and role-play the emotions involved and how to comfort each other.
7. **Classroom Helper:** Act out being a helper in the classroom, assisting others with tasks.
8. **Apologizing:** Role-play situations where an apology is needed and how to accept an apology.
9. **Cultural Celebration:** Role-play a cultural celebration, teaching about different traditions and respect.
10. **Feeling Scared:** Discuss and act out situations where someone might feel scared and how to offer comfort.

These activities and resources in Chapter 9 are designed to be interactive and engaging, providing a hands-on approach to teaching empathy and social-emotional skills. By incorporating these ideas into daily routines, parents and educators can create a rich learning environment that fosters kindness, understanding, and empathy in young minds.

Chapter X: Using Sign Language Activities and Signs to Promote Empathy and Kindness

Chapter 10 of "The Empathy Garden: Growing Kindness & Understanding in Young Minds" explores the use of sign language as a powerful tool for nurturing empathy and kindness in early childhood. Sign language, beyond its primary function as a communication method for the deaf and hard of hearing, offers unique opportunities for children to develop emotional intelligence and understanding.

Sign Language Usage Implementation

Introducing Sign Language in Early Childhood

We begin by highlighting the importance of introducing sign language at an early age. Young children are naturally adept at learning new forms of communication, and sign language can be both engaging and fun. This section includes practical tips for integrating basic sign language into daily routines and playtime. By learning signs for emotions such as happy, sad, angry, and scared, children can better express and recognize these feelings in themselves and others.

Activities to Enhance Empathy through Sign Language

This part of the chapter focuses on specific activities designed to use sign language as a medium to teach empathy. For instance, role-playing games where children use sign language to convey emotions help them step into others' shoes. We also suggest group activities where children must use signs to understand and respond to the feelings of their peers, fostering a sense of community and mutual respect.

Signs of Kindness: A Daily Practice

Here, we discuss how daily practice of sign language can be oriented towards expressions of kindness and compassion. Encouraging children to use signs for 'please', 'thank you', and 'sorry' not only teaches good manners but also instills a deeper understanding of these concepts. This section includes ideas for incorporating these signs into everyday classroom interactions, thus embedding kindness into the fabric of daily communication.

Resources and Further Learning

The chapter concludes with a curated list of resources for educators and parents. This includes recommended sign language courses, books, and online resources that are specifically designed for young learners. Additionally, we provide guidance on how to continuously incorporate sign language into the curriculum to ensure ongoing practice and learning.

Throughout the chapter, we emphasize the role of sign language in developing non-verbal communication skills, enhancing emotional literacy, and building a foundation for empathetic and kind interactions. By incorporating these practices into early childhood education, we can help cultivate a more understanding and compassionate generation.

The Benefits of Using American Sign Language (ASL) for Empathy and Kindness Learning and Skill Building

In this chapter of "The Empathy Garden: Growing Kindness & Understanding in Young Minds," we delve into the significant benefits of using American Sign Language (ASL) as a tool for fostering empathy and kindness in early childhood education.

1. **Enhanced Communication Skills**: ASL provides children with an alternative method of communication, empowering them to express themselves more fully and understand others better. This is particularly beneficial for children who may have difficulties with verbal communication.
2. **Improved Emotional Recognition**: Learning ASL includes understanding facial expressions and body language, which are key components of the language. This helps children become more attuned to recognizing emotions in themselves and others, fostering empathy.
3. **Inclusive Learning Environment**: Incorporating ASL in classrooms promotes inclusivity, especially for children who are deaf or hard of hearing. This inclusiveness teaches children about diversity and acceptance from a young age.
4. **Development of Fine Motor Skills**: The use of hand movements and gestures in ASL helps in the development of fine motor skills. These skills are crucial for early childhood development and academic tasks such as writing.
5. **Encourages Patience and Attention**: Learning and using ASL requires focus and patience, skills that are beneficial for children's overall cognitive development and interpersonal interactions.
6. **Building a Non-Verbal Communication Skillset**: ASL enhances children's ability to understand and use non-verbal cues, an essential part of empathetic interactions and understanding others' perspectives.

7. **Fosters a Sense of Community and Belonging**: Using a shared language like ASL can create a sense of community in the classroom, making children feel more connected and empathetic towards one another.
8. **Reduces Frustration and Encourages Expression**: ASL can be especially helpful for children who are not yet verbally articulate. It provides them with a means to express their needs and emotions, reducing frustration and promoting understanding.
9. **Enhances Memory and Cognitive Skills**: Learning a second language, including ASL, has been shown to improve memory, problem-solving skills, and critical thinking abilities in young children.
10. **Promotes Cultural Awareness and Sensitivity**: Teaching ASL introduces children to Deaf culture, fostering cultural sensitivity and awareness from a young age. This is a vital component of teaching empathy and kindness towards all individuals, regardless of their abilities or backgrounds.

In conclusion, the integration of ASL into early childhood education presents a multifaceted approach to nurturing empathy, kindness, and a range of cognitive and emotional skills. By embracing this form of communication, educators can provide a more inclusive, understanding, and empathetic learning environment for all children.

20 ASL Signs to Enhance Empathy and Kindness Learning and Skill Building

In "The Empathy Garden: Growing Kindness & Understanding in Young Minds," Chapter 10 focuses on the 20 most effective American Sign Language (ASL) signs that can be used to enhance empathy and kindness in early childhood education. Each sign is not only a tool for communication but also a step towards building a more compassionate and understanding mindset among young learners.

1. **Happy**: Cup your hand in front of your chest and brush it in an upward motion. This sign reflects a positive emotion, encouraging a cheerful atmosphere.
2. **Sad**: Run your fingers down your face from your eyes. This sign helps children express and recognize sadness, fostering empathy.

3. **Help**: Place your closed fist with the thumb up over an open palm and lift them together. This sign teaches the importance of offering and seeking assistance.
4. **Friend**: Link your index fingers together in a hooked motion. This sign represents friendship and encourages building connections.
5. **Please**: Rub your chest in a circular motion with a flat hand. This polite gesture promotes good manners and respect.
6. **Thank You**: Touch your chin with your fingers and move your hand away from your face. This sign is a basic expression of gratitude.
7. **Sorry**: Form a fist and rub it in a circular motion over your chest. This sign encourages taking responsibility and expressing remorse.
8. **Feel**: Point to your chest or touch your heart. This sign helps in expressing and identifying emotions.
9. **Share**: Move your hands forward with your palms up as if offering something. This sign promotes the concept of sharing and generosity.
10. **Kind**: Place your hand on your heart and then extend it outward. This sign symbolizes acts of kindness.
11. **Love**: Cross your arms over your chest as if giving yourself a hug. This sign represents love and affection.
12. **Angry**: Make a clawed hand and move it upward by your face. This sign helps children express and identify anger in a healthy way.
13. **Scared**: Place your hands open near your face and wiggle your fingers. This sign helps in expressing fear and understanding it in others.
14. **Listen**: Point to your ear. This sign encourages attentive listening and understanding.
15. **Patient**: Tap your hand with a finger, indicating the need to wait. This sign teaches the value of patience.
16. **Respect**: Flick your index finger off your forehead. This sign conveys the importance of respect towards others.
17. **Peace**: With both hands, form the letter 'V' and then move your hands down slightly. This sign symbolizes peace and harmony.

18. **Happy to Meet**: Smile and shake an imaginary hand in front of you. This friendly gesture encourages positive social interactions.
19. **Cooperate**: Link your index fingers, then move them in a circular motion together. This sign promotes teamwork and cooperation.
20. **Understand**: Point to your forehead and then flick your index finger outwards. This sign represents understanding and comprehension.

These 20 ASL signs provide a foundation for teaching important social and emotional concepts such as empathy, kindness, gratitude, and respect. By integrating these signs into daily interactions, educators can create a more inclusive, understanding, and compassionate learning environment.

Utilizing 10 Stories and 10 Songs to Promote and Enhance Empathy and Kindness Learning and Skill Building

In "The Empathy Garden: Growing Kindness & Understanding in Young Minds," Chapter 10 emphasizes the use of stories and songs as dynamic tools for teaching empathy and kindness. Integrating American Sign Language (ASL) into these activities not only enhances understanding but also provides a multisensory learning experience for young children.

10 Stories and ASL Signs to Use

1. **"The Giving Tree" by Shel Silverstein**

- ASL Sign: **Give** - Start with both hands in front of your chest, palms facing in, then extend them forward, palms up.

2. **"Have You Filled a Bucket Today?" by Carol McCloud**

- ASL Sign: **Kind** - Place your hand on your heart and then extend it outward.

3. **"The Invisible Boy" by Trudy Ludwig**

- ASL Sign: **Friend** - Link your index fingers together in a hooked motion.

4. **"Wonder" by R.J. Palacio**

- ASL Sign: **Respect** - Flick your index finger off your forehead.

5. **"A Sick Day for Amos McGee" by Philip C. Stead**

- ASL Sign: **Care** - Place both hands together at your chest, then move them outward.

6. **"The Lion and the Mouse" (Aesop's Fable)**

- ASL Sign: **Help** - Place your closed fist with the thumb up over an open palm and lift them together.

7. **"The Rainbow Fish" by Marcus Pfister**

- ASL Sign: **Share** - Move your hands forward with your palms up as if offering something.

8. **"Each Kindness" by Jacqueline Woodson**

- ASL Sign: **Change** - Form your hands into fists, then flip them over.

9. **"The Name Jar" by Yangsook Choi**

- ASL Sign: **Accept** - Start with your hands in front of your chest, palms facing you, and then open them outwards.

10. **"Chrysanthemum" by Kevin Henkes**

- ASL Sign: **Love** - Cross your arms over your chest as if giving yourself a hug.

10 Songs and ASL Signs to Use

1. **"If You're Happy and You Know It"**

- ASL Sign: **Happy** - Cup your hand in front of your chest and brush it in an upward motion.

2. **"This Little Light of Mine"**

- ASL Sign: **Light** - Open your hand, palm up, then flick your middle finger to your thumb, as if flicking on a light.

3. **"The More We Get Together"**

- ASL Sign: **Together** - Form a circle with both of your hands and bring them together.

4. **"Lean on Me" by Bill Withers**

- ASL Sign: **Support** - Place one hand under your other arm, as if holding it up.

5. **"What a Wonderful World" by Louis Armstrong**

- ASL Sign: **World** - Form a 'W' with your fingers and spin your hands around each other.

6. **"You've Got a Friend in Me" from Toy Story**

- ASL Sign: **Friend** - Link your index fingers together in a hooked motion.

7. **"Count on Me" by Bruno Mars**

- ASL Sign: **Count** - Tap your fingers as if counting.

8. **"It's a Small World"**

- ASL Sign: **Small** - Pinch your thumb and index finger together with your other fingers closed.

9. **"Let There Be Peace on Earth"**

- ASL Sign: **Peace** - With both hands, form the letter 'V' and then move your hands down slightly.

10. **"We Are the World" by USA for Africa**

- ASL Sign: **Together** - Form a circle with both of your hands and bring them together.

Each of these stories and songs, complemented by their corresponding ASL signs, stands as a valuable resource for instructing and reinforcing the principles of empathy, kindness, and understanding. The incorporation of ASL not only teaches children to express these values but also fosters a profound connection to the emotions and messages conveyed in these narratives and melodies.

Chapter XI

The Link Between Generosity and Growing Kindness

Welcome to Chapter XI of "The Empathy Garden: Growing Kindness & Understanding in Young Minds." In this chapter, we delve into the profound connection between generosity and the cultivation of kindness in early childhood.

Generosity, at its core, is the selfless act of giving without expecting anything in return. It can manifest in various forms – sharing toys, offering help, or even giving a smile. For young minds, understanding and practicing generosity is a stepping stone to developing a kind-hearted nature.

As we embark on this journey, let's explore how generosity is more than just sharing physical objects. It's about sharing time, attention, and empathy. When a child learns to give, they're not just parting with something; they're gaining an understanding of others' feelings and needs. This awareness is crucial in nurturing empathy, a key component of kindness.

We'll discuss practical activities and storytelling techniques that you can use to illustrate the joy of giving. These methods are designed to be engaging and relatable for young children, helping them grasp the concept of generosity in a fun and meaningful way.

Moreover, we'll examine the role of role models and the environment in reinforcing these values. Children learn by example, so it's vital that they see acts of generosity and kindness in their daily lives. This chapter will provide strategies for parents, caregivers, and educators to embody and encourage these traits.

Finally, we'll touch on the long-term benefits of instilling a generous spirit in children. From building stronger relationships to developing a sense of community and belonging, the impacts of generosity extend far beyond the early years.

By the end of this chapter, you will be equipped with the knowledge and tools to effectively foster a sense of generosity in young minds, thereby planting the seeds of kindness that will grow with them throughout their lives. Let's begin this rewarding journey together.

The Link Between Generosity and Growing Kindness: Incorporating Generosity Principles to Teach and Grow Kindness in Young Children

As an early childhood social-emotional educator, incorporating generosity principles into your teaching methods offers a multifaceted approach to cultivating kindness in young children. Generosity, in this context, extends beyond mere acts of giving; it encompasses a broader spectrum of behaviors that include sharing, empathizing, and acting selflessly. Here, we explore ten significant benefits of integrating these principles into early childhood education:

1. **Development of Empathy**: Teaching generosity helps children understand and respond to the feelings and needs of others. This empathy-building is essential for nurturing kind, compassionate individuals.
2. **Enhanced Social Skills**: Children who practice generosity learn valuable social skills such as sharing, cooperating, and taking turns. These skills are crucial for building healthy relationships both in childhood and later in life.
3. **Improved Emotional Intelligence**: Generosity aids in developing emotional intelligence, enabling children to better recognize, understand, and manage their own emotions and those of others.
4. **Building Self-Esteem**: Acts of generosity can boost a child's self-esteem. When children see the positive impact of their actions on others, they feel more confident and valued.

5. **Fostering a Sense of Belonging**: Generous behaviors promote inclusivity and a sense of belonging. Children learn to appreciate the value of being part of a community and contributing to its well-being.
6. **Encouraging Positive Behavior**: Generosity sets a foundation for other positive behaviors. Children who learn the value of giving are more likely to exhibit kindness, compassion, and understanding throughout their lives.
7. **Reducing Selfishness**: By focusing on the needs and feelings of others, children learn to overcome selfish tendencies, leading to more harmonious interactions with peers and adults.
8. **Enhancing Problem-Solving Skills**: Generosity often involves finding creative ways to help others. This can enhance problem-solving skills as children think of various ways to share, help, or collaborate.
9. **Cultivating Gratitude**: Generosity and gratitude are interlinked. When children learn to give and share, they also learn to be grateful for what they have and the kindness they receive from others.
10. **Long-Term Well-being**: The principles of generosity can have long-lasting effects on a child's mental and emotional well-being. Kind and generous individuals often lead more fulfilling and happier lives.

Incorporating these principles into early childhood education not only enriches the development of individual children but also plays a role in fostering a more compassionate, empathetic, and cooperative society. Teaching young children the significance of generosity lays the foundation for a future where kindness and understanding take center stage in human interactions.

As an early childhood social-emotional educator, using specific activities and strategies to teach the principles of generosity is a powerful way to foster kindness in young children. Here are ten strategies and activities, along with a selection of books and songs, that can be effectively incorporated into your teaching:

Strategies and Activities for Teaching Generosity and Kindness

1. **Sharing Circle**: Create a circle time where children are encouraged to share something with the group, whether it's a toy, an idea, or a story. This promotes sharing and listening skills.
2. **Role-Playing**: Use role-play scenarios to demonstrate acts of kindness and generosity. This helps children understand how their actions affect others.
3. **Kindness Calendar**: Develop a calendar with daily acts of kindness for children to complete, such as helping a friend or writing a thank-you note.
4. **Storytelling Sessions**: Regularly read stories that focus on themes of sharing and empathy, followed by group discussions on the moral of the story.
5. **Crafting for Others**: Engage children in crafting projects that are meant for others, such as making cards for family members or friends.
6. **Community Projects**: Participate in simple community service projects, like a neighborhood cleanup or a visit to a local nursing home.
7. **Empathy Role Reversal**: Encourage children to think about how others feel by asking them to put themselves in someone else's shoes.
8. **Generosity Jar**: Have a jar where children can add a token every time they do something kind. When the jar is full, celebrate with a special activity.
9. **Praise Generous Behavior**: Acknowledge and praise children when they display acts of kindness and generosity.
10. **Group Cooperation Games**: Use games that require teamwork and cooperation, emphasizing the importance of working together and helping each other.

Books on Generosity and Kindness

1. **"The Giving Tree" by Shel Silverstein**
2. **"Kindness is my Superpower" by Alicia Ortego**
3. **"Have You Filled a Bucket Today?" by Carol McCloud**
4. **"The Rainbow Fish" by Marcus Pfister**
5. **"A Chair for My Mother" by Vera B. Williams**
6. **"One Smile" by Cindy McKinley**

7. **"The Lion and the Mouse" by Jerry Pinkney**
8. **"Last Stop on Market Street" by Matt de la Peña**
9. **"The Invisible Boy" by Trudy Ludwig**
10. **"Stone Soup" by Marcia Brown**

Songs That Teach Generosity and Kindness

1. **"The More We Get Together" – Traditional**
2. **"It's a Great Day to Be Kind" – Jack Hartmann**
3. **"Kindness Counts" – Charity and the JAMband**
4. **"Give a Little Love" – Ziggy Marley**
5. **"Be Kind to Your Web-Footed Friends" – Traditional**
6. **"Count on Me" – Bruno Mars**
7. **"Respect" – Aretha Franklin**
8. **"What a Wonderful World" – Louis Armstrong**
9. **"Lean on Me" – Bill Withers**
10. **"Can You Feel the Love Tonight" – Elton John**

These books and songs are excellent resources for instilling the values of generosity and kindness in young children. They provide engaging and relatable content that makes learning about these important social-emotional skills enjoyable and memorable.

Chapter XII
Conclusion: A World of Empathy

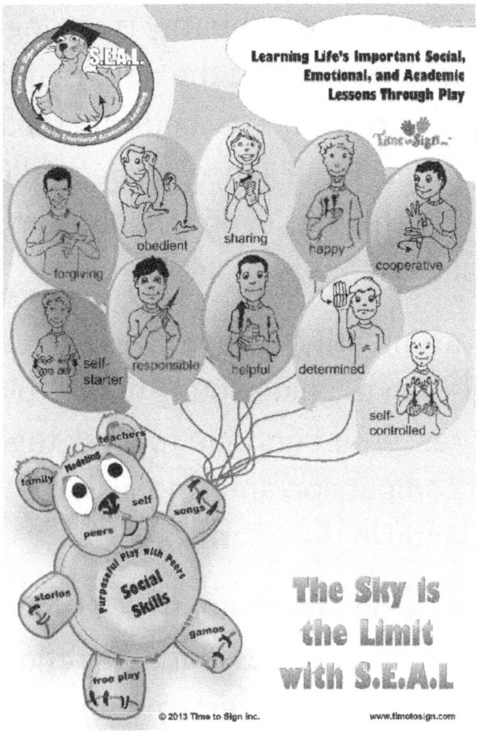

In this, the concluding chapter of "The Empathy Garden: Growing Kindness & Understanding in Young Minds," we contemplate the profound influence that nurturing empathy in early childhood can wield on both individuals and society. As educators and caregivers, we find ourselves on a remarkable journey, sowing seeds of kindness, understanding, and emotional intelligence in the fertile minds of young children. Throughout the pages of this guide, we've delved into diverse strategies and activities meticulously crafted to cultivate empathy, acknowledging it as a pivotal skill that enhances not only individual lives but also the broader community.

The Empathy Garden metaphor aptly captures our approach to teaching empathy. Just like a garden, empathy requires careful tending. It needs the right environment to flourish, including exposure to diverse perspectives, compassionate guidance, and opportunities for meaningful interactions. We've seen how empathy can grow from simple roots – understanding emotions, practicing active listening, and recognizing the value in others' experiences – to form a lush landscape of compassionate and empathetic individuals.

As we conclude this guide, it's important to acknowledge that the journey doesn't end here. The cultivation of empathy is an ongoing process, one that extends beyond the classroom and into the homes and communities of our children. By continuing to nurture these seeds of empathy, we are contributing to a world that values emotional intelligence, respects differences, and fosters a sense of global citizenship. This world, enriched by empathy, is one where kindness is not just an act, but a way of life.

We hope that "The Empathy Garden" serves as a lasting resource for you, offering tools and inspiration to guide young minds towards a more empathetic and understanding future. Let us continue to work together, nurturing the next generation in a spirit of compassion and kindness, creating a world where empathy blooms abundantly in the hearts of all.

As we draw to a close on "The Empathy Garden: Growing Kindness & Understanding in Young Minds," it is essential to reflect on the journey we have taken together. This guide has been a testament to the power of empathy in shaping the hearts and minds of our youngest generation. From the first chapter to the last, we have delved into the art and science of nurturing empathy, providing educators and caregivers with practical tools and insights to foster this critical skill in children.

The key lessons of the book revolve around the core principles of empathy: understanding and sharing the feelings of others, recognizing and respecting our differences, and responding with kindness and compassion. We explored activities that encourage emotional literacy, such as storytelling and role-playing, which help children understand and express their feelings. We highlighted the importance of modeling empathy as adults, showing children through our actions how to listen, care, and support others. We also discussed creating an inclusive environment where every child feels valued and heard, fostering a sense of belonging and mutual respect.

In summarizing these lessons, we reiterate that empathy is more than just a skill—it's a way of being. It's about creating a world where kindness is the norm, where understanding transcends barriers, and where compassion drives our actions.

To inspire children and adults to continue growing their empathy gardens, it's crucial to remember that empathy is a living, evolving practice. It doesn't end with the closing of this book. Instead, it's a journey that continues in everyday interactions. We encourage you to keep the spirit of "The Empathy Garden" alive in your classrooms, homes, and communities. Celebrate the small acts of kindness, nurture the moments of understanding, and cherish the connections that empathy brings.

As educators and caregivers, let's commit to being lifelong gardeners in the Empathy Garden, cultivating an environment where every child can blossom into empathetic, understanding, and kind individuals. Let this guide be a starting point, a seed from which a more empathetic and compassionate world can grow. Together, let's watch the garden of empathy flourish, transforming our world one child, one interaction, and one kind act at a time.

Signs to Use in Conjunction with the Empathy Garden Signs Concept

Common Classroom Phrases

more please - más por favor

more

please

nap time - tiempo de acostarse, siesta

nap

time

pay attention please - atención por favor, atentos por favor

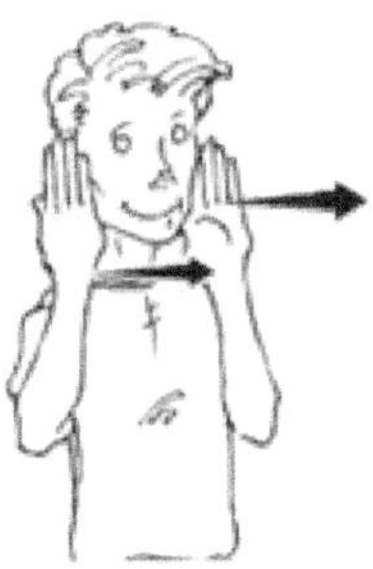

pay attention

please

Common Classroom Phrases

careful please - tengan cuidado por favor

careful please

please keep your hands to yourself - por favor, mantenga las manos quietas

please keep hands yourself

please sit still - sientese quieto por favor

please sit still

Common Classroom Phrases

please wait - espera por favor

wait

please

play time - tiempo de jugar

play

time

quiet please – silencio por favor

quiet

please

Common Classroom Phrases

say you are sorry
- digale que lo siento
- lo siento digale perdón, pidale perdón

say

sorry

I'm Sorry
- perdóname, disculpame

I'm

sorry

share please - compartír por favor

share

please

snack time - tiempo de comer un bocado, hora de la merienda

snack

time

stop now - parar ahora, pare ahora

stop

now

story time - tiempo de leer un libro de cuentos, tiempo de leer un cuento

story

time

time to eat - tiempo de comer, vamos a comer

time

eat

Common Classroom Phrases

time to go - vamonos

time

go

time to sign - tiempo de usar señales

time

sign

use your inside voices - use su voz de adentro

use

inside

voice

Common Classroom Phrases

use your manners - use sus modales

use

manners

use your words - use sus palabras

use

words

walk please - caminar, andar por favor

walk

please

wash your hands - lavarse sus manos

wash hands

Emotions

<table>
<tr><td>afraid - temeroso, susto, miedo, alarmar
Hold both open hands in front of the chest, palms facing the body, fingers pointing towards each other, slightly shaking hands.

[Also: scared, frightened, terrified]</td><td></td></tr>
<tr><td>angry - colérico
Place the curved "5" handshapes against the waist and draw up against the sides of the body.

[As if anger is boiling up out of person]

[Also: wrath]</td><td></td></tr>
<tr><td>bored – nada que hacer
Place the tip of the dominant index finger against the side of the nose and twist the finger slightly.

[As if picking one's nose]

[Also: boring, tedious, dull]</td><td></td></tr>
<tr><td>happy- alegre, feliz
With the open dominant hand pat the chest several times with a slight upward motion. Sign can also be done with both hands.

[As if heart is pounding with joy]

[Also: glad, rejoice, joy]</td><td></td></tr>
<tr><td>hurt - dolor
The index fingers are moved toward each other several times.

[Also: pain, ache]</td><td></td></tr>
</table>

Emotions

like - gustarle Place the dominant hand thumb and the middle finger against the chest (other fingers separated) and draw them away from the body, closing the two fingers.	
love – amor, cariño The "S" handshapes are crossed at the wrist and pressed to the heart. [As if hugging one's self]	
sad - triste Hold both open hands in front of the face, fingers slightly apart and pointing up; then drop both hands a short distance and bend the head slightly. [Also: dejected, sorrowful, downcast]	
tired - cansado Fingertips of the bent hands are placed at each side of the body just above the waist and then dropped slightly. [Also: weary, exhausted]	
upset (crying) - llorar Draw the index fingers down the cheeks from the eyes several times. [Also: cry, weep, tears]	

goodbye – adios Start with the dominant open hand straight in front of the body, palm facing forward and hand pointing up, bend the fingers up and down in a repeated movement.	
good morning – buenos dias Bring the dominant "5" handshape from the mouth down to the upward turned palm of the reference palm in front of the chest. Then with the reference open hand in the crook of the bent dominant arm, bring the dominant open handshapes upward, palm facing in.	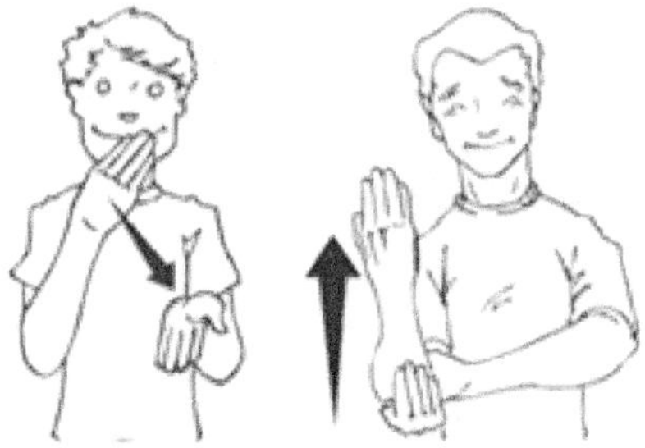
hello – hola Start with the fingertips of the dominant "B" handshapes near the side of the forehead, palm angled slightly forward, move the handshapes forward in a deliberate movement.	

How are you?
Coma estas?

Fine,
bien

okay
bastante
bien, okay

how **you** **fine** **"O"** **"K"**

Manners

excuse me – disculpame, perdóname, con permiso Brush the fingertips of the dominant open hand across and off of the little finger side of the upturned reference hand.	
good – bueno, bien Starting with fingertips of the open dominant hand on the lips, move the hand down to touch the open palm. [As if something tasted good and you want more]	
manners – modales Tap the thumb of the dominant "5" handshape, with a double movement, against the chest.	
may I – puedo yo/mi Start with both "S" handshapes in front of the chest, palms facing down, move both hands downwards simultaneously with a short double movement. Then point the extended index-finger of the dominant hand to the center of the chest.	
no – no Bring the dominant index-finger, middle finger and thumb together in one motion.	

Manners

please – por favor Rub the chest with the open dominant hand in a circular motion (palm facing yourself) [As if rubbing your heart] [Also: pleasure, enjoy]	
thank you - gracias Touch lips with the fingertips of flat dominant hand, then move the hand forward until the palm is facing up and towards the indicated person. [Smile and nod head while doing this sign]	
welcome – bienvenido, de nada/no hay de qué Bring the upturned dominant curved hand from in front of the dominant side of the body in toward the center of the waist.	
yes - sí Shake the dominant "S" handshape up and down in front of you.	

Questions

<table>
<tr><td>ask - preguntar
Bring the palms of both open hands together, fingers angled upward, while moving both hands up and in towards the chest.

[Natural gesture for saying please in asking]</td><td></td></tr>
<tr><td>how – cómo
Beginning with the knuckles of both curved hands touching in front of the chest, palms facing down, twist the hands upward and forward, ending with the fingers together pointing up and the palms facing up.</td><td></td></tr>
<tr><td>question - pregunta
Start with the extended dominant index finger in front of the dominant shoulder, move the dominant hand down with a curved movement while retracting the index-finger, then extending it again at the bottom of the curve.

[As if drawing a question mark in the air]</td><td></td></tr>
<tr><td>what – qué
Bring the extended index-finger of the dominant hand down across the reference open hand striking the fingers as they are passed.</td><td></td></tr>
<tr><td>when – hasta, cuando
Move the extended index-finger of the dominant hand in an arc to touch the extended index-finger of the reference hand in front of the reference hand side of the body.

[Also: until]</td><td></td></tr>
</table>

Made in the USA
Middletown, DE
31 March 2024

52327828R00051

MUJER AMBICIOSA

MENTALIDAD PARA EL ÉXITO

Glenda Martínez

Dedicación

Sergio Pino 🕊

Hoy me despido de ti con el corazón lleno de gratitud y admiración. Tu presencia en mi vida fue una luz guía, un faro de inspiración y fortaleza que siempre me mostró el camino. Fuiste más que un primo; para mí, fuiste un mentor. Eras la unión y unidad de nuestra familia, un pilar en los momentos más difíciles y un apoyo inquebrantable en mis logros.

Cada paso que doy, cada meta que alcanzo, lleva tu huella. Me ayudaste a creer en mis sueños y a luchar por ellos con determinación y pasión. Sin tu sabiduría y tu ejemplo, no sería la persona que soy hoy. Tu legado vive en mí y en todos aquellos que tuvieron la fortuna de conocerte y aprender de ti.

Hoy te despido con lágrimas, pero también con la promesa de honrar tu memoria continuando con el trabajo que empezamos juntos. Tu espíritu de excelencia y tu compromiso con el éxito seguirán siendo mi norte.

Gracias por todo lo que me diste, por cada enseñanza y cada palabra de aliento. Descansa en paz, Sergio Pino. Tu legado de inspiración y amor nunca será olvidado.

Nacido en La Habana, Cuba, en 1956 – fallecido en 2024, Miami, Florida. Con todo mi cariño y eterna gratitud, en nombre de tu Familia Burgos-Pino.

Cabe destacar que, en mi primer proyecto de libro, él envió una lista detallada de 50 personas que querían que este libro fuera un regalo de su parte. En nombre de Sergio Pino, Mujer Ambiciosa va por ti.

Sergio Pino y Glenda Martínez

Glenda Martínez Burgos
Autora de Mujer Ambiciosa

MUJER EMPRENDEDORA

Mentalidad para el éxito

INTRODUCCIÓN

Bienvenido a "Womanpreneur Mindset for Success", una guía diseñada para la mujer ambiciosa y con visión de futuro lista para embarcarse en un viaje de descubrimiento y crecimiento empresarial. Este libro es más que una simple recopilación de estrategias comerciales; es un viaje al corazón de lo que significa ser mujer en el mundo del emprendimiento.

En estas páginas encontrará no sólo ideas y consejos prácticos, sino también inspiración y empoderamiento. Cada capítulo está diseñado para abordar los desafíos y oportunidades únicos que enfrenta como mujer emprendedora. Desde descubrir sus motivaciones principales y alinear su negocio con sus pasiones hasta abrazar su fuerza interior y superar las dudas, este libro es su compañero en el camino hacia el éxito.

Entonces, ya sea que recién esté comenzando o esté buscando redefinir su trayectoria empresarial, "Womanpreneur Mindset for Success" está aquí para guiarla, inspirarla y empoderarla. Comencemos este viaje juntos, explorando las profundidades de nuestro potencial y las alturas de nuestras aspiraciones. Bienvenido a un mundo de posibilidades, crecimiento y éxito. Bienvenido a "Mentalidad de mujer emprendedora para el éxito".

AUTOR

Abraza la idea de darte un capricho con regalos especiales, llenar tu vida de amor y recibir una generosidad ilimitada. Sueña tan grande como tu corazón desee. Eres digno de eso. Prosperidad. Riqueza. Bienestar. Logro. Una vida exitosa te está llamando. Reclamarlo. Confía en ello. Entra en ello. Personificarlo. Haga estas afirmaciones parte de su rutina diaria: Mi negocio está generando ganancias sustanciales. El dinero fluye hacia mí con facilidad, lo que me permite tener una vida llena de éxito y satisfacción. ¡Soy la personificación del éxito! El éxito es sinónimo de mí. Crea una vida que te apasione. Visualízalo. Fomentarlo. Experimentalo.

Persigue tus sueños y hazlos realidad. Tienes el poder de dar forma a tu futuro. Confía en lo que puedes hacer y persigue lo que quieres sin miedo. Recuerda, tú estás a cargo de tu historia. Viva con valentía y nunca se arrepienta de apuntar alto. Recorre tu camino con confianza y encuentra alegría en las cosas que muestran tu verdadero yo. Construya una vida en la que sus creencias allanen el camino hacia el éxito y pongan el listón alto. Haz crecer tu confianza en ti mismo hasta tal punto que la opinión de nadie pueda sacudirte. Mantente orgulloso de tu propio ser maravilloso.

Mi nombre es Glenda Martínez Burgos, nacida en La Habana, Cuba. Desde muy pequeñita me trasladaron a España, a las Islas Canarias, Tenerife, donde me crie y nació mi vocación por la estética. Desde 2007, me convertí en cosmetóloga profesional y desde entonces me he dedicado al mundo de la belleza.

Actualmente vivo en los Estados Unidos, en Miami, donde encontré la inspiración para ser lo que soy ahora: una instructora que ayuda a otras personas a seguir el mismo camino y alcanzar el éxito. Hoy en día, si no estamos creciendo, estamos retrocediendo. Por ello, para nosotros y para la Academia GMB Institute, que es nuestra motivación diaria, es fundamental que ustedes se conviertan en mejores profesionales cada día.

Contamos con más de 25 estados, más de 40 distribuidores y tres líneas profesionales, de las cuales estamos muy orgullosos, tanto del equipo como del trabajo que hemos realizado hasta ahora. La Academia GMB Institute nació en 2018 con la motivación absoluta de que cada profesional pueda cumplir su sueño.

De mí, te diré que siempre se puede. Soy mamá de dos maravillosos niños, esposa, madre, hija, amiga, y nunca existe la posibilidad del «no puedo», «no lo voy a lograr» ni «no lo voy a conseguir». El éxito sí existe, pero debemos ser más sofisticados en cómo hacemos las cosas. Quien se prepara y visualiza lo que quiere percibe mucho mejor las oportunidades. Como bien dijo Pablo Picasso, la inspiración sí existe, pero debe encontrarnos trabajando.

Testimonios

¿Qué podemos plasmar aquí que no sepa quién te conoce? Mujer incansable, guerrera, luchadora, amiga, hija, esposa y, sobre todo, madre. Tienes el don de hacer que todo parezca fácil, incluso cuando sé que detrás de cada escena has trabajado incansablemente para lograrlo. Ejemplo de ello es este bello libro lleno de vivencias y fuerza para mujeres luchadoras. Por eso, tus hijos y yo vivimos orgullosos de quién eres y del camino recorrido hasta aquí. Nunca soltaremos tu mano y caminaremos juntos en esto que se llama vida. Te amamos, eres increíble.

Alberto Cora (esposo)

Haber conocido a Glenda Martínez en 2018 fue un privilegio que transformó mi vida tanto en lo profesional como en lo personal. Desde entonces, he sido parte de su equipo y cómplice de su crecimiento, dedicación y apoyo continuo. Glenda enfrenta cada desafío como una oportunidad de crecimiento; para ella, la palabra «no» no existe. Más allá de su impresionante visión y determinación, tiene una manera especial de conectar con las personas, contagiándonos su energía para motivarnos y hacernos creer en nuestras propias capacidades. Nos enseña que los únicos obstáculos son los que nosotros mismos ponemos, y que verdaderamente no existen cuando se quiere alcanzar algo. Glenda no solo es una profesional excepcional, sino también un ejemplo de crecimiento y perseverancia.

Como amiga, puedo decir que siempre ha estado incondicionalmente presente. Cada día junto a ella ha sido una lección de resiliencia y determinación. Me ha apoyado en cada momento difícil y me ha recordado que el camino hacia nuestros sueños está lleno de oportunidades para crecer y triunfar. ¡Te adoro!

Alyanaid Preciado

Compañera y amigo de trabajos por muchos años

UNA MUJER QUE APUESTA POR LO MEJOR

La vida de la mujer de hoy desafía los estereotipos que limitan su rol, encajonándola solo en su desempeño como esposa y madre. Su papel ha cambiado y ha marcado un nuevo patrón de comportamiento social, sacándola de una esfera privada y colocándola de manera activa en la esfera pública, donde se ha posicionado exitosamente como líder profesional, empresaria, figura pública, entre muchas cosas más.

Tal es la historia de Glenda Martínez, una mujer apasionada por su misión de vida y con la determinación y fuerza para conquistar todo. Glenda es una cosmetóloga internacional, esteticista e instructora de formación profesional con una extensa trayectoria y un amplio currículum de estudios. Es una orgullosa madre y esposa que ha sabido combinar estas obligaciones con su deseo interminable de éxito. Su mayor anhelo es ser el ejemplo y la inspiración de todas las mujeres que, como ella, sueñan día a día con cumplir todas sus metas. Acompáñenme a conocer más a esta extraordinaria mujer que siempre apuesta por lo mejor.

Dios perfecciona tus pasos a través de tus caídas y solo hace que te conviertas en un gran estratega que sabe dónde y cuándo apostar. (Glenda Martínez)

Entrevista

¿Cómo ha sido tu trayectoria profesional en el mercado de la belleza y la medicina estética?

Soy GM de Belle Institute, una escuela reconocida en los Estados Unidos por ser pionera en tratamientos novedosos del mercado estético europeo y americano. Cuento con 16 años de experiencia en este campo, desde que comencé en 2007. Soy cosmetóloga certificada en España, en las Islas Canarias, donde me crie durante 23 años, aunque nací en Cuba.

De nacimiento, soy cubana, pero me trasladaron a España cuando era muy pequeña, donde estudié y descubrí mi vocación. Cuento con más de 16 años de experiencia en medicina estética, con una única misión: ayudar a otros a luchar por sus profesiones y sueños.

Además, soy la CEO de Belle Skin y Oxylif, marcas cosméticas para uso profesional, compuestas por formulaciones avanzadas en estética. Oxylif es una patente a nivel mundial, con una fórmula única en el mundo, vegana, fabricada en España, en Alicante, en la Universidad de Valencia. Contamos con una red de distribución y comercialización en muchos países de Centroamérica y Latinoamérica, así como en todos los Estados Unidos y España.

¿Qué es lo que más te satisface de lo que haces?

Sin duda, ver a las personas crecer es mi mayor satisfacción. No solo es mi pasión en la estética, sino que también actúo como psicóloga. Observo a mis alumnos y saco el potencial que hay en ellos para tareas específicas. Mi principal función es simplificar, enseñar y abrirles un camino, sobre todo a nivel mental. Identifico el talento en cada persona y les muestro las herramientas necesarias. Desde pequeña, siempre he dado todo lo que tengo y sé. Damos lo que somos, y ese es mi verdadero ser.

¿Qué retos has tenido que enfrentar como mujer de negocios?

Sin duda, mi mayor reto fue convertirme en mamá durante mi crecimiento profesional. Cuando estaba en pleno auge, me quedé embarazada de mi primer hijo, y esto no me detuvo en absoluto; el embarazo no fue una traba para mí.

El embarazo, lejos de ser una excusa para quedarme en casa, me impulsó a trabajar más. No dejé de trabajar ni un solo momento. Continué con mi profesión, atendiendo clientes, y además aprendí y vendí en el ámbito corporativo multinivel, destacándome en ventas. Esto me permitió seguir adelante y aprender sobre cómo una mujer puede ganarse la vida, incluso durante el complicado proceso del embarazo.

Sin duda, este fue el reto más duro que he enfrentado, y no lo hubiera logrado sin el apoyo de mi familia y el gran hombre que tengo a mi lado, el papá de mis hijos y mi esposo actual. No solo soy mamá de un niño, sino también de una niña. Ambos tienen actualmente seis y cuatro años. Se llevan muy poco tiempo, pero uno de mis mayores sueños en la vida siempre fue formar una familia.

Antes de convertirme en una mujer exitosa, siempre quise tener una familia y brindarles a mis hijos seguridad, tranquilidad y una vida plena, algo que quizás uno anhela cuando no tiene a sus padres unidos, como es mi caso, ya que fui criada por padres separados.

Así que eso siempre fue lo que anhelé para mi familia, y he logrado complementar esto con mi carrera, mis viajes y los éxitos alcanzados. Tuve la oportunidad de quedarme en casa y retomar mis labores una vez que terminé, ya que realmente nunca enfrenté problemas económicos en esos momentos; trabajar no era una obligación para mí, pero esa no fue mi decisión.

Continué estudiando y trabajando, y aunque uno de mis sueños era quedarme en casa criando a mis hijos, complementé todo a la perfección. Sabía que uno de mis hijos era mi razón de ser, y quería que fueran fuertes, saludables y felices. Esto dependía más del amor familiar que del tiempo que pudiera brindarles.

Mi esposo y padre de los niños me apoyó y se convirtió en el superhéroe que respaldó a mamá en todos sus sueños, eventos y viajes logrados hasta hoy.

¿Cuáles fueron los hábitos que te han llevado a ser una empresaria tan exitosa?

Estar y aprovechar los momentos adecuados. Cuando tienes el conocimiento y el talento, lo más importante es colocarte en una posición estratégica para que las oportunidades lleguen a ti. Las grandes oportunidades existen, pero deben encontrarte trabajando.

¿Quién es la madre, la esposa, madre e hija que te inspiró a ser la mujer que eres?

Sin duda, mi mamá. Podría pasar horas hablando de su gran labor en el mundo y de su trayectoria, pero la realidad es que lo que realmente me inspiró fue su ejemplo como madre, hija, esposa, hermana y trabajadora. Ella estudió una carrera a los 20 años y una profesión a los 50. Me mostró que quien quiere puede, sin importar la edad ni la situación. Siempre me sacó adelante, me ayudó a superar situaciones incómodas y me llevó a países donde realmente podía prosperar y tener éxito. Mi mamá, sin duda, es mi mayor ejemplo de fortaleza.

¿Qué representan los miembros de tu familia en tu éxito empresarial?

Para mí, lo representan todo, porque aunque es cierto que hay personas que surgen de las peores situaciones y aun así tienen éxito, creo firmemente que quienes logran un éxito más contundente, más fuerte y duradero en el tiempo son aquellos que están rodeados de un entorno familiar estable y saludable.

Un entorno familiar estable y saludable no es algo que se da por hecho; uno lo crea, lo conquista o ya lo tiene. Algunos lo tenemos, otros lo conquistan y algunos lo crean. Pero cuando tienes un entorno saludable a tu alrededor, ya sea con padres, abuelos, esposos o hijos saludables, puedes dedicarte a tu éxito, desarrollar ideas y triunfar.

Uno no puede crear y tener ideas, ni estar completamente enfocado en el éxito si no tiene un entorno estable. Cuando no tienes un entorno estable, tu vida es inestable, y eso dificulta el avance. Una mujer de éxito debe procurar que su entorno sea el adecuado; es por ahí por donde debemos comenzar. Aunque uno piensa que debe empezar por uno mismo, el entorno familiar es crucial para el éxito empresarial. Después de tantos años y escribiendo este libro, estoy convencida de que el entorno familiar es fundamental.

Cuando hablo de entorno familiar, me refiero a tus amigos, tu mamá, tu papá, tu esposo, tus hijos. La manera en que enseñas a las personas a tratarte es la forma en que tú mantendrás tu estabilidad emocional. Una persona puede tener éxito en algunos días, una temporada o un tiempo en un entorno inestable, pero ese éxito no será duradero.

El éxito a largo plazo se construye en un entorno tranquilo, donde puedes dormir suficientes horas sin preocuparte por gritos, conflictos o resolver los problemas de los demás. El entorno familiar influye mucho porque, como te decía, somos como un jardín. Si el jardín no tiene abono, no crecerá ni florecerá. Pero si está abonado y estable, entonces florecerás. Por lo tanto, el entorno familiar es primordial para el crecimiento y el éxito.

Así que, una persona que desea tener éxito, aunque le toque la lotería o reciba la mejor noticia del mundo, primero debe revisar su entorno. ¿Dónde estoy? ¿Cuál es mi jardín? ¿Estoy bien? ¿Floreceré aquí? ¿Las personas a mi alrededor están contentas y felices con lo que hago? Si la respuesta es no, es necesario salir de ese entorno para florecer en otro lugar. Si la respuesta es sí, entonces se requiere trabajar más para lograr lo que deseas.

En mi caso, procuré que mi entorno familiar y la familia que he creado sean de paz y salud. Esto me permite tener mis horas de sueño, tiempo para mí y dedicarme a otras personas. Sin duda, esto fue clave para todo lo que he logrado hoy: mantener mis empresas, crear marcas y dedicarme a otros. Puedo enfocarme en el crecimiento y el consejo de otras personas porque tengo una vida estable, un entorno familiar estable, un esposo, una mamá y unos hijos que admiran a su mamá, a su hija y a su esposa, y me lo demuestran cada día.

De esta manera, puedo ayudar a otros a florecer porque yo estoy floreciendo. Las personas heridas necesitan personas sanas para sanar. Como coach en 2024, me dedico a guiar a empresas y mujeres por esta razón. Al estar sana, puedo enseñar desde la tranquilidad cómo debes posicionarte, cómo debes ser tratada para ser feliz y cómo encontrar las herramientas para tener éxito. Una mujer feliz, que hace algo que le apasiona, siempre encontrará las herramientas para triunfar.

¿Qué haces para equilibrar las responsabilidades de tu empresa y de tu familia en tu vida personal?

Cuando abro los ojos a las 5 de la mañana, porque soy del grupo de las 5 de la mañana, creo fielmente que entre las 4 y las 5 de la mañana es el mejor momento para ayudar, tener ideas, resolver y organizar mi vida. Cuando vivimos nuestro día en bloques de tiempo, podemos aprovechar al máximo lo que queremos lograr.

Así, a las 5 de la mañana, desgloso las tareas de mi día. Siempre mantengo una agenda y no admito planes inesperados o fuera de la agenda. Normalmente trato de seguir mi planificación, y esto ha sido uno de los beneficios que me ha llevado al éxito.

Trato de maximizar cada hora, y cuando llega la tarde, es el tiempo de mi familia. Entre las 4 y las 5 de la tarde, estoy con mis hijos, cocino, hago actividades con ellos, vamos a pasear, salimos en la patineta, y, como me levanté a las 4 de la mañana y realicé todas mis tareas laborales, no llego a las 6 de la tarde con retrasos en mi trabajo. Aproveché el día y completé mis tareas por la mañana. Si fuera una persona que se levanta a las 11 de la mañana, es muy probable que todavía tuviera trabajo a las 10 de la noche, ya que no adelanté mis tareas y no tendría tiempo para dedicar a mis hijos. Dedico mucho tiempo a mis hijos, estoy con ellos, viajo con ellos, y el tiempo que paso con ellos es lo más importante en mi vida.

¿Cómo te ves en el futuro?

Me visualizo viajando por el mundo entero con mis hijos, conociendo ciudades y coleccionando atardeceres, y sin duda, aprendiendo de mentoras y ejemplos de tantas mujeres que necesitan un empuje para comenzar. Me apasiona ayudar a otras personas y así quiero llegar a mis últimos días, sabiendo que con mis palabras, mi labor o mi ejemplo, alguien ese día no se rindió. Quiero demostrar a todos que sí se puede tener éxito siendo migrante, joven, con dos hijos, sin capital previo, empezando desde cero y trabajando. Si yo pude, tú también puedes lograrlo.

¿Cuál es tu propósito y misión de vida?

Mi propósito es ser un ejemplo de superación en el mundo actual. Quiero ser alguien real, con una vida real, que pueda decir: «sí, tú puedes, vamos a hacerlo».

Mi misión es mejorar cada día lo que hago para que la gente también lo logre. Sentir que solo una persona en el mundo ha conquistado algo gracias a mí me hace sentir orgullosa y creo que he cumplido mi misión.

¿Cuáles son tus tres claves para el éxito personal?

Las tres claves para obtener éxito personal son la disciplina, el enfoque y la estrategia. Ninguna de estas claves incluye el talento, porque el talento es algo innato. Pero si no desarrollas disciplina, enfoque y estrategia, el talento nunca se desarrollará. Puedes nacer con un talento y morir con él si no tienes disciplina, enfoque y estrategia. Sin estos elementos, nunca te enterarás de que tenías un talento y, por lo tanto, nunca lo desarrollarás.

Disciplina

La primera etapa del desarrollo es la disciplina, ni siquiera la motivación. Estamos motivados hoy, pero mañana no. La motivación es efímera, dura muy poco. No podemos trabajar solo con motivación, sino con disciplina. Cuando no quieres hacer algo, lo haces, aunque estés cansada. Eso es una de las ayudas que tuve. Uno no se levanta todos los días motivado, por lo que la disciplina es lo único que te queda para ganar.

Enfoque

Si no tienes claro lo que quieres, probablemente perderás mucho tiempo tratando de tener éxito en todo. Desde muy joven supe lo que quería y aproveché mi pasión por la belleza, la estética y el maquillaje para ayudar a otras personas a sentirse bien. Aproveché esa pasión junto con la disciplina y el enfoque para encaminarme. A lo largo de los años, me ofrecieron muchos trabajos y oportunidades que rechacé para mantenerme en la estética. Ahora tengo una escuela, un resultado del mismo enfoque, ya que una cosa me llevó a la otra: de la estética a crear una escuela y de la escuela a desarrollar marcas profesionales con patentes.

Estrategia

Sin duda, la estrategia es fundamental. Si no tienes estrategia junto con disciplina y enfoque, tampoco llegarás a ningún lado. Conozco muchas personas que tienen disciplina y están enfocadas, pero que carecen de estrategia. Ahí es donde encontramos debilidad. No dan pasos hacia las oportunidades. Cada año, cada día, se presentan oportunidades, pero debes crearlas. Las oportunidades no llegan solas, debes salir a buscarlas, conocer a más personas y estar en lugares donde puedas encontrarlas.

Por ejemplo, si te dedicas al mundo de la belleza o la estética, yo asisto a más de 10 eventos de estética cada año buscando oportunidades. Las oportunidades no llaman a tu puerta. Si te dedicas al sector inmobiliario, debes asistir a eventos relacionados. Si trabajas en el mundo del libro, debes participar en eventos de publicación y firmas de libros. Sea cual sea tu campo, debes estar presente en los lugares que fomentan tu carrera, porque ahí es donde están las oportunidades.

No saber aprovechar las oportunidades es una debilidad común. Para obtener el contrato, el dinero o la oportunidad de tu vida, debes estar en el momento preciso. Una persona exitosa es aquella que no se rindió, que fue a muchas oportunidades, y un día recibió ese contrato, esa oportunidad o esa guía para finalmente alcanzar el éxito que buscaba.

¿Cómo te has preparado para el éxito?

Quien se prepara y visualiza lo que quiere, percibe mucho mejor las oportunidades. La persona que cree que lo sabe todo, en realidad no sabe nada. Somos eternos aprendices y, prácticamente hasta el día en que muramos, tendremos que seguir aprendiendo. Estudiar, aprender de otros y de cualquier mínima cosa es una de las herramientas más importantes para cualquier persona que quiera tener éxito.

Por eso, es crucial estudiar y ejecutar ideas. Digamos que soy la cabeza ejecutora de cada paso en la empresa, por lo que estudio el mercado, las ideas, las probabilidades y las herramientas necesarias para que todo funcione. Si no tenemos las herramientas, las busco para que el proyecto sea exitoso. En mi tiempo libre, no veo series; leo libros sobre cómo ganar más clientes, mentalidades millonarias, ideas transformadoras o incluso el libro negro.

Considero que mi éxito proviene de mi labor diaria y de lo que hago día a día para que las oportunidades beneficien a mi empresa.

¿Qué consejo le das a las mujeres que aspiran a ser empresarias exitosas?

Lo que me funcionó a mí no necesariamente te funcionará a ti, porque la vida te prepara una ecuación matemática diferente para cada persona. Sin embargo, si tuviera que ofrecer un consejo que sirva para todos los seres humanos en cualquier momento, sería uno de mi escritor favorito: «no intentes agradar a todo el mundo, o perderás el respeto de todos».

Busca a tus amigos y tu gente entre aquellos que están convencidos de lo que hacen y de lo que son. No digo que busques a alguien que piense igual que tú, sino a alguien que piense diferente y al que nunca podrás convencer de que tú tienes la razón. La amistad, el amor y el éxito no se basan en opiniones; acepta los desafíos incondicionalmente.

No intentes hacer cualquier cosa a cualquier precio, porque ser una persona buena para el mundo no tiene precio. El éxito no es la misma ecuación para todos; cada uno tiene un diferenciador y un ADN único.

Es muy importante tener, número uno, un entorno saludable; número dos, disciplina, enfoque y estrategia. Cuando complementas estos elementos y los repites constantemente, lograrás aquello que consideres éxito, ya que el éxito significa cosas diferentes para cada persona. Al final, manifestarás que has llegado a un punto en tu vida en el que estás haciendo lo que te gusta, provocando lo que te gusta, ganando dinero y viviendo según tus pasiones. Para muchas personas, eso ya es el éxito.

Capítulo 07

SUPERAR LAS DUDAS SOBRE UNO MISMO

Capítulo 08

SUPERAR EL MIEDO AL FRACASO

Capítulo 09

LIBERARSE DEL PERFECCIONISMO

Capítulo 10

DE LA COMPARACIÓN A LA INSPIRACIÓN

Capítulo 11

CONSTRUYENDO UNA HERMANDAD SOLIDARIA EN LOS NEGOCIOS

Capítulo 12

CREAR UNA VISIÓN PERSONAL DEL ÉXITO

Capítulo 13

CÓMO LANZAR TU NEGOCIO DIGITAL EN 30 DÍAS

01 CAPÍTULO UNO

DESCUBRIENDO SU "POR QUÉ" EN LOS NEGOCIOS

Bienvenido al comienzo de un viaje transformador, un viaje en el que descubrirá las motivaciones y pasiones centrales que impulsarán su aventura empresarial. Estoy encantado de guiarte en este proceso de autodescubrimiento que, créeme, es tan apasionante como crucial en el mundo de los negocios.

¿Por qué empezar con "por qué"? Porque saber tu 'por qué' es como tener una brújula en el desierto; guía tus decisiones, te mantiene concentrado y te recuerda por qué empezaste cuando las cosas se ponen difíciles. Es el corazón de la historia de su negocio, el pulso detrás de cada esfuerzo que realiza.

Empecemos por quitar las capas. ¿Qué te motiva? No se trata sólo de ganancias. Piensa más profundamente. ¿Es un deseo de crear algo propio? ¿Un sueño para marcar la diferencia en tu comunidad? O tal vez sea la libertad y flexibilidad que conlleva ser tu propio jefe. Tu "por qué" es únicamente tuyo, un tapiz tejido a partir de tus experiencias, sueños y valores.

Ahora, reflexiona sobre lo que te apasiona. ¿Qué enciende ese fuego en tu corazón? Podría ser cualquier cosa: un pasatiempo, una causa, una idea persistente que te mantiene despierto por la noche. Cuando su negocio se alinea con lo que realmente le importa, no sólo prospera; resuena con autenticidad, atrayendo clientes y oportunidades que se alinean con sus valores.

Descubriendo su "por qué" en los negocios

Está bien si tu "por qué" evoluciona con el tiempo. Todos estamos en un viaje y el cambio es parte del crecimiento. La clave es permanecer conectado con tu brújula interior, dejando que guíe tu camino a través del apasionante mundo del emprendimiento.

Descubre tu por qué

Profundicemos en un ejercicio de reflexión personal para descubrir su "por qué", el corazón de su impulso empresarial. Este viaje a sus experiencias pasadas tiene como objetivo revelar los patrones y valores que han dado forma a sus motivaciones.

Mientras reflexiona, observe las actividades, valores o temas recurrentes. Estas son las pistas de tu "por qué", la esencia detrás de tus pasiones y objetivos. Este proceso no se trata de respuestas correctas o incorrectas, sino de una autoexploración honesta.

Al escuchar la narrativa de tus experiencias, descubrirás las motivaciones que impulsan tu camino empresarial, ofreciendo una visión más clara de lo que te motiva. Esta nueva comprensión sienta las bases para un negocio que no sólo es exitoso sino que también es un verdadero reflejo de usted.

Paso 1: Reflexionar sobre los momentos de satisfacción

Piensa en momentos de tu vida, tanto personal como profesional, en los que te sentiste realmente satisfecho. ¿Que estabas haciendo? ¿Con quién estabas? ¿Qué pasa con estos momentos que los hicieron tan satisfactorios?
Escriba estas experiencias e intente identificar los hilos comunes que las vinculan. Podría ser la sensación de logro, creatividad, conexión o algo completamente distinto.

Paso 2: Identifique los logros que más le enorgullecen

Ahora, cambie su atención a sus logros. de que estas mas orgulloso? Estos pueden ser grandes o pequeños, desde lanzar un proyecto exitoso hasta ayudar a un amigo necesitado. Considere por qué estos logros se destacan para usted. ¿Es el impacto que tuvo, las habilidades que utilizó o los desafíos que superó?

Paso 3: Recordar tiempos de cumplimiento genuino

Ahora, cambie su atención a sus logros. de que estas mas orgulloso? Estos pueden ser grandes o pequeños, desde lanzar un proyecto exitoso hasta ayudar a un amigo necesitado. Considere por qué estos logros se destacan para usted. ¿Es el impacto que tuvo, las habilidades que utilizó o los desafíos que superó?

CONTAR HISTORIAS

Al elaborar esta guía, considero esencial compartir con ustedes una parte de mi propia historia, un vistazo a mi viaje para descubrir mi "por qué". Esta narrativa personal no es sólo un recuento de experiencias; es una ilustración de cómo los conceptos que hemos discutido cobran vida en el mundo real.

Mi camino para comprender mi "por qué" no fue una línea recta. Fue un camino sinuoso, lleno de momentos de claridad, confusión y profunda realización. Como muchos emprendedores, mi empresa comenzó con una pasión, un deseo ardiente de crear algo significativo. Pero la pasión por sí sola no fue suficiente para sostener el largo viaje que tenía por delante. Necesitaba profundizar más, comprender la fuerza impulsora detrás de esta pasión.

Al principio, mi atención se centraba principalmente en los aspectos externos del negocio: las estrategias, el marketing, los números. Si bien estos son sin duda importantes, pronto me di cuenta de que eran sólo una parte de la ecuación. Lo que realmente importó, lo que realmente me sostuvo a través de desafíos y reveses, fue la razón subyacente de mi esfuerzo: mi "por qué".

Descubrir mi "por qué" fue un proceso introspectivo. Implicaba retirar capas de ambiciones, aspiraciones y sueños para descubrir el núcleo de lo que me motivaba. Se trataba de alinear mi negocio con mis valores personales, entendiendo que lo que hago es un reflejo de quién soy y en qué creo.

Este viaje de autodescubrimiento no fue sólo esclarecedor; fue transformador. Cambió la forma en que abordé las decisiones comerciales, interactué con los clientes e imaginé el éxito. Mi "por qué" se convirtió en la brújula que guió mis estrategias, la lente a través de la cual vi las oportunidades y el ancla que me mantuvo firme.

Compartir este viaje contigo no se trata sólo de transparencia; se trata de forjar una conexión. Al revelar mi camino, espero inspirarte a embarcarte en tu propio viaje de autodescubrimiento, a encontrar tu "por qué" único y a ver cuán profundamente puede moldear tu enfoque de los negocios y la vida. A medida que profundizamos en esta guía, lo invito a reflexionar sobre mi historia, a encontrar paralelos en su propio viaje y a utilizar estos conocimientos como trampolín para su propia exploración. Recuerde, descubrir su "por qué" es un viaje que vale la pena emprender, un viaje que define no sólo su negocio, sino también su identidad como Mujer Emprendedora.

Ella construye su imperio
sobre los cimientos
De la confianza en sí misma
el coraje y una visión
inquebrantable del éxito.

Su ambición no conoce límites

La psicología del "por qué"

En nuestra exploración del espíritu emprendedor, es invaluable profundizar en los conocimientos psicológicos que subrayan la importancia del propósito y la motivación para impulsar tanto el éxito como la realización en los negocios. Comprender estos fundamentos psicológicos no sólo nos ilumina sobre el "por qué" detrás de nuestras acciones, sino que también nos guía para aprovechar estas fuerzas de manera efectiva.

El campo de la psicología revela que tener un sentido claro de propósito es más que una simple herramienta de motivación; es un factor clave para mantener el compromiso y la satisfacción a largo plazo en cualquier esfuerzo, especialmente en los negocios. El propósito actúa como una estrella del norte, guiando a los emprendedores a través de la incertidumbre y brindando un sentido de significado a su trabajo. Este sentido de propósito es a menudo lo que diferencia una carrera satisfactoria de un simple trabajo.

Además, la motivación, en particular la motivación intrínseca, desempeña un papel fundamental en el éxito empresarial. La motivación intrínseca (el impulso que surge desde dentro, impulsado por la satisfacción y el interés personal) suele estar vinculada a una mayor creatividad, resiliencia y persistencia. Es el tipo de motivación que mantiene a un emprendedor en marcha incluso en ausencia de recompensas o reconocimiento inmediatos, impulsando la innovación y el compromiso a largo plazo.

La investigación psicológica también arroja luz sobre el concepto de "flujo", un estado de profunda inmersión y disfrute en el trabajo. Es más probable lograr un estado de fluidez cuando participa en tareas que se alinean con su "por qué", sus valores e intereses fundamentales. Este estado no sólo aumenta la productividad sino que también contribuye a la felicidad general y la satisfacción laboral.

Comprender la psicología detrás del establecimiento de objetivos puede tener un impacto significativo en su trayectoria empresarial. Los objetivos bien definidos y motivados por un propósito proporcionan una dirección clara y, al mismo tiempo, permiten la flexibilidad necesaria para adaptarse y crecer. Ofrecen una sensación de logro y progreso, factores clave para mantener la motivación y combatir el agotamiento.

Los líderes eficaces son aquellos que comprenden no sólo la mecánica de los negocios sino también el elemento humano: las motivaciones, aspiraciones y comportamientos de ellos mismos y de su equipo. Un líder que está en sintonía con su propio propósito y motivaciones puede inspirar lo mismo en su equipo, creando una fuerza laboral cohesionada y motivada.

Tu Identidad

En el mundo del emprendimiento, hay un elemento clave que une tu pasión y tu propósito: el vínculo entre tu "por qué" y tu identidad de marca. Comprender esta conexión es crucial. Ayuda a crear una marca que realmente conecta con sus clientes y lo distingue en el mercado.

Su "por qué" es la razón principal detrás de la existencia de su empresa. Es más que una simple declaración de misión o un plan de negocios; es el latido del corazón de tu marca. Este "por qué" encarna sus pasiones, valores y la perspectiva única que aporta a su industria. Cuando esta esencia se infunde en la identidad de su marca, se crea una narrativa que es a la vez auténtica y convincente.

: En un mundo saturado de mensajes de marketing, la autenticidad no es sólo una palabra de moda; es un faro que guía a los clientes hacia su marca. Los clientes de hoy son inteligentes; buscan marcas que sean genuinas y alineadas con sus valores. Cuando la identidad de su marca refleja su verdadero "por qué", se forma una conexión más profunda con su audiencia, una conexión que se extiende más allá de las transacciones para generar una lealtad duradera.

Su "por qué" diferencia su marca de la competencia. No es sólo lo que haces o cómo lo haces, sino el por qué lo haces lo que cautiva a tu audiencia. Una narración efectiva que comunica este "por qué" en cada aspecto de su marca, desde su logotipo hasta su servicio de atención al cliente, lo distingue. Transforma tu marca de un mero producto o servicio a una historia en la que los clientes quieren participar.

La consistencia es clave

La coherencia al expresar su "por qué" en todos los canales solidifica la identidad de su marca. Ya sea a través de su sitio web, redes sociales o empaque, cada punto de contacto debe reflejar su mensaje central. Esta coherencia garantiza que, sin importar cómo o dónde los clientes interactúen con su marca, experimenten los mismos valores y mensajes fundamentales, lo que refuerza su identidad de marca.

A medida que su negocio crece, su "por qué" podría evolucionar. Es importante revisar periódicamente y posiblemente perfeccionar la identidad de su marca para asegurarse de que se mantenga fiel a su "por qué" actual. Esta evolución es una parte natural del crecimiento y mantiene su marca relevante e identificable.

Al construir su marca sobre la base de su "por qué" único, no solo crea un negocio, sino un legado que resuena con autenticidad y propósito. Deje que esta comprensión le guíe mientras da forma a una marca que realmente refleje quién es usted y qué representa en el mundo de los negocios.

Una verdadera Mujer Emprendedora
no espera las oportunidades
Ella las crea
con confianza y enfoque

02

CAPÍTULO DOS

CONVERTIR LA PASIÓN EN GANANCIAS

Convertir la pasión en ganancias

Convertir lo que amamos en un medio de vida es un sueño que muchos de nosotros compartimos. No estamos hablando sólo de ganar dinero aquí; Nos sumergimos en cómo crear una vida llena de pasión y satisfacción, una vida en la que tu trabajo sea una extensión de lo que enciende tu corazón.

Primero, hablemos de pasión. La pasión es esa chispa dentro de ti que se enciende cuando haces algo que amas. Es esa actividad o causa que te hace perder la noción del tiempo, que te hace sonreír y encender tu corazón. Ahora, imagina convertir esa pasión en tu medio de vida. Suena de ensueño, ¿no? Pero es absolutamente posible.

La clave aquí es identificar cómo tu pasión resuelve un problema o satisface una necesidad. Aquí es donde su pasión se encuentra con el mercado. Quizás tu amor por el arte pueda transformarse en un negocio de diseño gráfico. Quizás su talento natural para la organización pueda conducirle a un servicio de conserjería personal. Su pasión por la alimentación saludable podría convertirse en un servicio de planificación de comidas. Las posibilidades son infinitas.

Pero seamos realistas: la pasión por sí sola no es suficiente. Debe ir acompañado de un plan de negocios sólido, un conocimiento profundo de su público objetivo y una estrategia sobre cómo llegar a él. Esto puede parecer desalentador, pero no te preocupes, estamos juntos en esto.

Mientras navegamos por este proceso, recuerde que su perspectiva única y su toque personal son los que diferenciarán su negocio. En un mundo donde hay casi de todo para todos, tu autenticidad es tu mayor activo. Deje que su pasión brille en todos los aspectos de su negocio, desde su marca hasta su servicio al cliente y los mismos productos o servicios que ofrece.

Además, prepárese para una curva de aprendizaje. Transformar la pasión en ganancias es un viaje lleno de éxitos y desafíos. Aprovéchelos como oportunidades para hacer crecer y perfeccionar su negocio. Manténgase abierto a la retroalimentación, esté dispuesto a adaptarse y mantenga siempre su pasión en el centro de lo que hace.

El éxito es gustarte a ti mismo, que te guste lo que haces y que te guste cómo lo haces.

CERRAR LA BRECHA ENTRE UNA PASIÓN Y UN NEGOCIO EXITOSO ES COMO EMBARCARSE EN UNA BÚSQUEDA DEL TESORO. SABES LO QUE TE ENCANTA HACER, PERO LA CLAVE ES ENCONTRAR EL PUNTO ÓPTIMO DONDE TU PASIÓN SE ENCUENTRA CON UNA NECESIDAD DEL MERCADO. ASÍ ES COMO PUEDES NAVEGAR ESTE EMOCIONANTE VIAJE:

1 IDENTIFICAR LA NECESIDAD DEL MERCADO

Empiece por preguntarse: "¿Cómo sirve mi pasión a los demás?" Tal vez su amor por la repostería pueda traer alegría a las personas de su comunidad, o su entusiasmo por el ejercicio físico pueda ayudar a otros a alcanzar sus objetivos de salud. Tu pasión debe resolver un problema o satisfacer una necesidad por la que la gente esté dispuesta a pagar.

2 INVESTIGA A TU AUDIENCIA

¿Quién se beneficiará más de tu pasión? Comprender a su público objetivo es fundamental. Profundice en sus datos demográficos, intereses y puntos débiles. Esta información le ayudará a adaptar sus ofertas a sus necesidades y preferencias específicas.

3 IDENTIFICAR LA NECESIDAD DEL MERCADO

¿Cómo ganarás dinero con tu pasión? Hay varios modelos a considerar, como vender productos, ofrecer servicios, suscripciones u organizar talleres. Elija un modelo que se alinee con su pasión y sea factible dentro de su mercado objetivo.

4 CONSTRUYA UNA MARCA CON FUERTE IDENTIDAD

Su marca debe reflejar su pasión y resonar en su público objetivo. Desde su logotipo hasta sus materiales de marketing, cada elemento debe contar su historia y mostrar lo que hace que su negocio sea único.

5 CREAR UNA PRESENCIA EN LÍNEA

En el mundo digital actual, tener presencia en línea es vital. Un sitio web, perfiles de redes sociales y quizás un blog o podcast pueden ayudarlo a llegar a una audiencia más amplia y conectarse con los clientes.

6 PLAN DE SOSTENIBILIDAD

La pasión te ayuda a empezar, pero necesitas un plan sólido para seguir adelante. Elabore un plan de negocios que cubra cómo ganará dinero, cómo hará correr la voz y cómo crecerá. Mantenga la realidad sobre lo que costará y cuánto puede ganar. De esta manera, su pasión puede convertirse en un negocio duradero.

7 NUNCA DEJES DE APRENDER

El mundo empresarial siempre está evolucionando y usted también debería hacerlo. Manténgase actualizado sobre las tendencias de la industria, asista a talleres y busque tutoría. El aprendizaje continuo le ayudará a adaptarse y hacer crecer su negocio de forma eficaz.

8

RED Y COLABORACIÓN

Establecer relaciones con otros emprendedores puede abrir puertas a nuevas oportunidades. La creación de redes puede proporcionar apoyo, asesoramiento y posibles asociaciones. Estas relaciones pueden convertirse en un recurso poderoso, que ofrece nuevas perspectivas y abre caminos hacia el crecimiento y el éxito mutuos.

03 CAPÍTULO TRES

CREANDO UNA MENTALIDAD ORIENTADA AL ÉXITO

ELABORAR UNA ESTRATEGIA ORIENTADA AL ÉXITO

La forma en que aborda mentalmente su negocio puede influir significativamente en su éxito. No se trata sólo de mantener una perspectiva positiva; se trata de desarrollar una mentalidad que acepte los desafíos, acepte el cambio y persevere a través de los inevitables altibajos de los negocios. Profundicemos en cómo se puede cultivar esta mentalidad resiliente y adaptativa.

Abrazar la positividad: comience fomentando una perspectiva positiva. Esto no significa ignorar los desafíos o los reveses. Más bien, se trata de mantener una actitud esperanzada y optimista para superarlos. El pensamiento positivo abre tu mente a nuevas posibilidades y soluciones, algo crucial para cualquier emprendedor.

Desarrollar la resiliencia: la resiliencia es la capacidad de recuperarse de los contratiempos. Como emprendedor, enfrentará una buena cantidad de desafíos, pero lo que cuenta es cómo responde a estos desafíos. La resiliencia consiste en aprender de los fracasos y no dejarse vencer por ellos.

Adaptarse al cambio: la única constante en los negocios es el cambio. Cultivar una mentalidad adaptable significa estar abierto a nuevas ideas, cambiar estrategias cuando sea necesario y mantenerse ágil frente a las tendencias cambiantes del mercado.

Recuerde, siempre hay margen de mejora. Estar abierto a la retroalimentación y dispuesto a realizar cambios es crucial para el crecimiento y el éxito.

Establecer metas realistas: Establecer metas es esencial, pero es importante establecer metas alcanzables y realistas. Divida sus objetivos más importantes en tareas más pequeñas y manejables. Celebre las pequeñas victorias a lo largo del camino: se suman a logros importantes.

Cultivar una mentalidad de crecimiento: adopte el concepto de mentalidad de crecimiento. Esto significa creer que tus habilidades e inteligencia se pueden desarrollar con el tiempo. Una mentalidad de crecimiento conduce al amor por el aprendizaje y a una resiliencia que es esencial para lograr grandes logros.

Practicar la atención plena: estar presente y atento le ayuda a mantenerse concentrado y reduce el estrés. Le permite tomar decisiones más reflexivas y mejora su capacidad para afrontar los desafíos del día a día.

Aprender de los demás: no evite buscar consejo y aprender de aquellos que han recorrido el camino antes que usted. Los mentores, compañeros emprendedores e incluso los competidores pueden proporcionar información valiosa.

Manténgase comprometido con su visión: nunca pierda de vista su "por qué": la razón por la que inició su negocio. Esta visión lo mantendrá anclado y motivado, especialmente en tiempos difíciles.

El cuidado personal es crucial: por último, nunca subestimes el poder del cuidado personal. Un cuerpo y una mente sanos son sus mayores activos. Priorice su bienestar para mantenerla.

Persigue tus sueños y hazlos realidad. Tienes el poder de dar forma a tu futuro. Confía en lo que puedes hacer y persigue lo que quieres sin miedo. Recuerda, tú estás a cargo de tu historia. Viva con valentía y nunca se arrepienta de apuntar alto. Recorre tu camino con confianza y encuentra alegría en las cosas que muestran tu verdadero yo. Construya una vida en la que sus creencias allanen el camino hacia el éxito y pongan el listón alto. Haz crecer tu confianza en ti mismo hasta tal punto que la opinión de nadie pueda sacudirte. Mantente orgulloso de tu propio ser maravilloso.

04 CAPÍTULO CUATRO

EL VIAJE HACIA EL AUTODESCUBRIMIENTO EN LOS NEGOCIOS

VIAJE HACIA EL AUTODESCUBRIMIENTO EN LOS NEGOCIOS

Iniciar su viaje de autodescubrimiento en los negocios es realmente una aventura emocionante para comprenderse mejor a sí mismo. No se trata sólo de los pasos que usted da para desarrollar su negocio; se trata de descubrir quién eres realmente y de qué eres capaz como emprendedor y líder.

Al comenzar, tómate un momento para evaluar tus fortalezas y debilidades. Este no es sólo un ejercicio de autoconciencia; es un paso fundamental para aprovechar aquello en lo que eres bueno y reconocer dónde podrías necesitar apoyo o mayor desarrollo. Se trata de lograr un equilibrio entre la autoaceptación y el impulso de mejorar.

Su viaje empresarial es tan único como su huella digital. Es fácil caer en la trampa de comparar tu camino con el de otros, pero recuerda, tu viaje es sólo tuyo, completo con sus giros y vueltas únicos. Cada paso, cada decisión y cada experiencia es una lección en sí misma que contribuye a su crecimiento y resiliencia.

Este viaje es también una lección de liderazgo. El liderazgo no es igual para todos; es una expresión personal. Explora diferentes estilos y filosofías y, a través de tus experiencias, encuentra el que resuena contigo, se alinea con tus valores y habla de tu visión.

Alinear sus valores personales con su negocio es crucial. Es esta alineación la que inyecta propósito e integridad a su trabajo. Su negocio se convierte en algo más que un simple emprendimiento; se convierte en un reflejo de tus creencias y aspiraciones.

La reflexión es una herramienta poderosa en este viaje. Tómate un tiempo periódicamente para reflexionar sobre tus experiencias, tus decisiones y la dirección de tu negocio. Ya sea a través de un diario, la meditación o conversaciones con mentores, la reflexión ayuda a aclarar sus pensamientos y enfocar sus objetivos.

Manténgase abierto al crecimiento y al cambio. A medida que usted evolucione, también lo hará su negocio. Acepte esta evolución como una oportunidad para explorar nuevas vías y posibilidades para su negocio.

Con cada paso de este viaje, su confianza crecerá. Celebre cada logro, por pequeño que sea. Utilícelos como trampolines para desarrollar un sentido más fuerte de confianza en uno mismo.

Una mente curiosa es el combustible para la innovación y el crecimiento. Mantenga su curiosidad sobre su industria, sus clientes y, lo más importante, sobre usted mismo. Esta curiosidad mantiene su negocio dinámico, relevante y en constante evolución.

Por último, mantente conectado con tu yo interior. Comprende qué te motiva, qué te inspira y qué te desafía. Esta conexión interna es su brújula más confiable en el, a menudo, impredecible mundo del espíritu empresarial.

Este viaje de autodescubrimiento no se trata sólo de construir un negocio exitoso; se trata de crear una vida que sea rica, significativa y un verdadero reflejo de quién eres. Abracemos este viaje juntos, celebrando al emprendedor único que hay en cada uno de nosotros y descubriendo todo el alcance de nuestro potencial.

05

CAPÍTULO CINCO

LIBERANDO TU FUERZA INTERIOR COMO MUJER EMPRENDEDORA

LIBERANDO TU FUERZA INTERIOR

como mujer emprendedora

Cada mujer posee una combinación única de resiliencia, sabiduría y fuerza interior. Cuando estas cualidades se adoptan y utilizan plenamente, tienen el poder de convertir los desafíos empresariales en triunfos y victorias notables.

La resiliencia en las empresas implica mucho más que simplemente hacer frente a los fracasos; se trata de navegarlos con sabiduría, gracia y una mentalidad de aprendizaje. Cada desafío que enfrentas no solo fortalece tu resiliencia sino que también te proporciona una experiencia invaluable para futuros obstáculos. Este proceso de superar los desafíos y aprender de ellos proporciona una base sólida que lo guía a través de las complejidades del emprendimiento con un sentido de confianza, claridad y previsión estratégica.

Confiar en sus capacidades constituye la piedra angular de un emprendimiento exitoso. Se trata de reconocer tus habilidades y experiencias, y comprender cómo te preparan para tomar decisiones acertadas y liderar de manera efectiva. Esta confianza se traduce en una tranquilidad que resuena con fuerza en el mundo empresarial.

Tu inteligencia emocional es un activo vital. Le permite forjar conexiones profundas con los clientes, empatizar con su equipo y navegar hábilmente en las negociaciones. Esta capacidad de comprender y gestionar las emociones va más allá de la compasión; es una herramienta estratégica para construir relaciones y crear una base de clientes leales, combinando agudeza emocional con conocimiento empresarial.

El poder de una Mujer Emprendedora no reside sólo en cómo gestiona su negocio, sino en cómo supera sus miedos con gracia.

Abrace su perspectiva única. Sus experiencias individuales, antecedentes culturales y conocimientos personales le permiten ver oportunidades y soluciones que otros podrían perder, lo que distingue a su empresa en un mercado competitivo.

El coraje para asumir riesgos es parte integral del crecimiento empresarial. Ya sea lanzar un nuevo producto, ingresar a un nuevo mercado o cambiar su modelo de negocio, estas decisiones audaces lo llevarán más allá de su zona de confort, fomentando el crecimiento y experiencias de aprendizaje invaluables.

Su estilo de liderazgo es una expresión de su personalidad. Ya sea enriquecedor, colaborativo o visionario, ser dueño de su estilo marca la pauta para su cultura empresarial y dinámica de equipo, y resuena con aquellos que comparten sus valores.

Fomentar la confianza en uno mismo consiste en reconocer y aprovechar los logros. Esta creencia no solo alimenta su fuerza interior, sino que también moldea la forma en que los demás lo ven y responden, impulsando su capacidad para tomar decisiones impactantes y elevar su negocio.

Equilibrar la fuerza con la compasión es clave para un liderazgo eficaz. Esta combinación garantiza que se tomen decisiones difíciles cuando sea necesario, mientras que la empatía y la comprensión mantienen un ambiente de trabajo saludable y productivo.

MANTENTE ERGUIDO EN TU GRANDEZA ÚNICA

Mantenerse fiel a uno mismo en los negocios significa alinear sus prácticas con sus valores y ética personales.

La autenticidad en sus interacciones y la transparencia en sus tratos atraen a clientes, socios y empleados que comparten su visión, creando un negocio que no sólo es exitoso, sino también un fiel reflejo de sus ideales.

Su viaje como Mujer Emprendedora es una combinación de estas cualidades, cada una de las cuales agrega su tono y textura únicos a la obra maestra que es su negocio.

El activo más poderoso en su viaje empresarial es su yo auténtico, su autenticidad inquebrantable. Acéptalo, celébralo y deja que sea la fuerza que te guíe en tu camino hacia el éxito, dando forma a un negocio que sea tan único e impactante como tú.

TU ÉXITO SE MIDE EN MOMENTOS DE AUTENTICIDAD

06

CAPÍTULO SEIS

EL PODER DE LA INTUICIÓN EN LOS NEGOCIOS

El poder de la intuición en los negocios

En el competitivo mundo del emprendimiento, tu intuición es como una brújula secreta que te guía a través de decisiones grandes y pequeñas. Es ese presentimiento, la voz interior que susurra ideas que quizás no encuentres en los datos o las tendencias. En este capítulo, exploramos cómo aprovechar su intuición puede cambiar las reglas del juego en su trayectoria empresarial.

La intuición en los negocios a menudo se subestima, pero es una profunda fuente de sabiduría. Es una combinación de sus experiencias, conocimientos e ideas, destilados en un sentimiento o corazonada. Piense en ello como su mente subconsciente, que procesa información y patrones más rápido que su mente consciente. Aprender a confiar e interpretar esta intuición puede llevarlo a tomar decisiones que estén sincronizadas con sus objetivos y valores más profundos.

Aprovechar la intuición comienza con la sintonización. En el ajetreo de las tareas y decisiones diarias, tómate un momento para escuchar tu voz interior. ¿Qué dice? A menudo, nuestra primera

reacción instintiva ante una situación o decisión tiene sus raíces en una comprensión profunda de nuestros verdaderos deseos y miedos. Reconocer este instinto puede resultar increíblemente revelador.

Pero, ¿cómo se diferencia entre intuición e impulso? La intuición no es un capricho pasajero; es un mensaje coherente que proviene de un lugar de sabiduría y comprensión. Se basa en sus experiencias pasadas y el conocimiento de su negocio. Los impulsos, por otra parte, suelen ser reacciones a emociones o deseos inmediatos. Aprender a distinguirlos es crucial.

La intuición también juega un papel en la comprensión de los demás, ya sean clientes, socios o miembros del equipo. Le ayuda a leer entre líneas, detectar preocupaciones tácitas y evaluar la sinceridad de las personas con las que interactúa. Esto puede resultar especialmente valioso en negociaciones, contrataciones y creación de asociaciones.

Integrar la intuición con la toma de decisiones racional es la clave. Si bien la intuición puede guiarlo, equilibrarla con un análisis lógico garantiza decisiones integrales. Utilice su intuición para identificar posibles oportunidades o problemas y luego utilice datos y análisis para verificar y planificar su curso de acción.

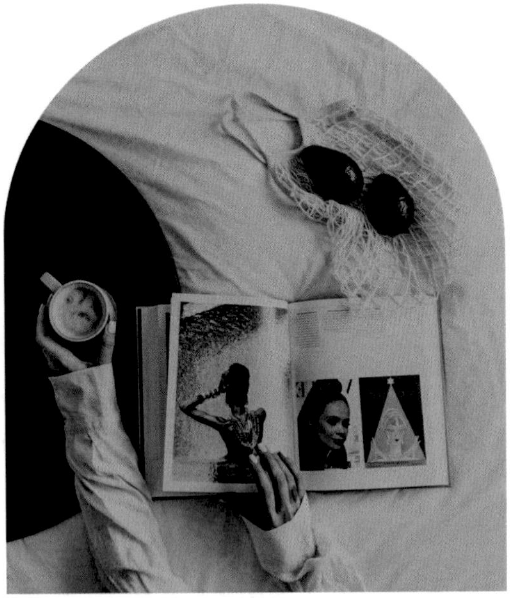

Cultivar tu intuición es como cultivar una relación

Confiar en su intuición en los negocios también significa estar preparado para ir contra la corriente.

A veces, lo que intuitivamente parece correcto puede no ser lo que se hace tradicionalmente.

Podría significar tomar un camino poco convencional o tomar una decisión que otros tal vez no comprendan inicialmente. Pero recuerde, algunas de las empresas más exitosas se construyeron a partir de decisiones que inicialmente desafiaron la lógica.

Cultivar tu intuición es como cultivar una relación. Requiere paciencia, comprensión y confianza. Cuanto más escuches y actúes según tu intuición, más fuerte y clara se vuelve. Se trata de construir un vínculo con tu yo interior, comprendiendo que esta sabiduría interior es un actor clave en tu viaje empresarial.

Su intuición es una herramienta poderosa en su arsenal empresarial. Mejora su conocimiento, experiencia y análisis, aportando una dimensión más profunda a su proceso de toma de decisiones. Aprovechar y confiar en esta intuición no es sólo empoderante; es una ventaja estratégica en el complejo mundo de los negocios. Permita que su intuición lo guíe y lo ayude a tomar decisiones que resuenen con sus valores y visiones más profundos para su camino empresarial.

EL MÉTODO SILVA
Para la intuición

El Método Silva, desarrollado por José Silva en la década de 1966, es un programa de autoayuda diseñado para aumentar las capacidades del individuo a través de la relajación, el desarrollo de funciones cerebrales superiores y capacidades psíquicas como la intuición.

El núcleo del Método Silva implica aprender a entrar en un estado relajado, conocido como estado de ondas cerebrales alfa, que se cree que es más propicio para el aprendizaje, la curación y la concentración en objetivo.

> Mejore la intuición estando presente, notando señales sutiles y confiando en su voz interior para guiar su camino.

El Método Silva abarca diversas técnicas y ejercicios, que incluyen visualización, meditación y ensayo mental. A los profesionales se les enseña a visualizar o imaginar los resultados deseados, lo que se cree que influye positivamente en su capacidad para lograr estos resultados en la realidad.

El Método SILVA

Un componente clave del Método Silva es el desarrollo de la intuición. El programa sugiere que al aprender a relajarse y sintonizarse con el estado alfa, los individuos pueden acceder a más potencial de su cerebro, mejorando sus habilidades intuitivas. Estas habilidades luego se pueden utilizar para tomar mejores decisiones, resolver problemas y pensar creativamente.

Otros aspectos clave del Método Silva incluyen:

Meditación y Relajación: El método enfatiza la importancia de la relajación profunda y la meditación. Enseña técnicas para calmar la mente y entrar en un estado de relajación profunda, que se cree que facilita el acceso a más potencial del cerebro.

Entrenamiento de ondas cerebrales alfa y theta: El Método Silva se centra en entrenar a las personas para que entren conscientemente en estados de ondas cerebrales alfa y theta. Se cree que estos estados, típicamente asociados con la relajación profunda y la meditación, mejoran la creatividad, el aprendizaje, la memoria y la intuición.

Visualización y ensayo mental: a los participantes se les enseña a usar la visualización y la imaginación para ensayar mentalmente los resultados exitosos de los desafíos que enfrentan. Esta práctica tiene como objetivo mejorar el desempeño en diversos aspectos de la vida, incluyendo el ámbito personal y profesional.

Pensamiento positivo y afirmaciones: el método fomenta el uso de pensamientos y afirmaciones positivas para reforzar los objetivos y mejorar el bienestar mental y emocional general.

El Método Silva ha sido popular en los círculos de autoayuda y se ha utilizado para diversos fines, incluida la reducción del estrés, la mejora de la creatividad, la salud y el aumento de la productividad. Sin embargo, es importante señalar que algunas de las afirmaciones hechas por el Método Silva, especialmente aquellas relacionadas con las habilidades psíquicas y los efectos de los estados de ondas cerebrales, no son universalmente aceptadas ni respaldadas por la investigación científica convencional. Como ocurre con cualquier programa de autoayuda, las experiencias y los resultados individuales pueden variar. Sin embargo, muchas personas han encontrado valor en sus técnicas para la relajación, la reducción del estrés y el desarrollo personal.

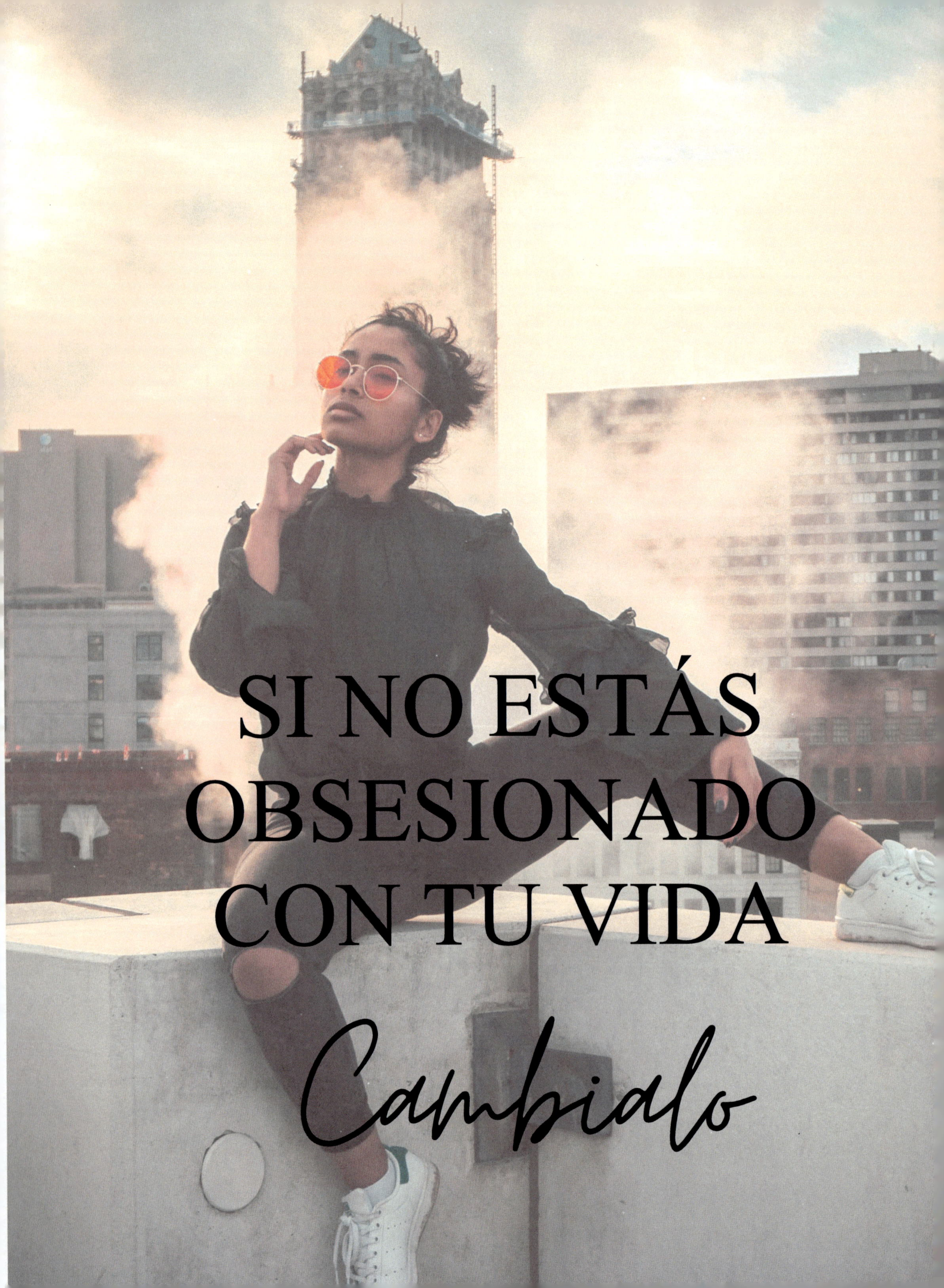
SI NO ESTÁS
OBSESIONADO
CON TU VIDA
Cambialo

07 CAPÍTULO SIETE

SUPERAR LAS DUDAS SOBRE UNO MISMO

VENCIENDO DUDAS

En su viaje empresarial, la duda es una encrucijada familiar, un punto donde la incertidumbre se encuentra con la posibilidad. Es una parte natural del proceso, especialmente cuando estás explorando nuevos territorios. Sin embargo, superar estas dudas es esencial para avanzar con confianza y éxito. Este capítulo trata sobre cómo convertir las dudas en uno mismo en confianza en uno mismo.

La duda a menudo aparece cuando enfrentamos nuevos desafíos o salimos de nuestra zona de confort. Se manifiesta en preguntas como "¿Soy lo suficientemente bueno?" o "¿Qué pasa si fallo?". El primer paso para superar las dudas sobre uno mismo es reconocerlas como una respuesta normal al crecimiento y al cambio. No es un reflejo de tu capacidad o potencial.

Reconocer sus logros es un poderoso antídoto contra las dudas. Reflexiona sobre tus éxitos pasados, por pequeños que sean. Cada uno es una prueba de tu capacidad y resiliencia. Éstas no son sólo victorias pasadas; son recordatorios de su potencial para lograr aún más.

Construir una red de apoyo puede ser increíblemente útil para superar las dudas. Rodéate de mentores, compañeros y amigos que crean en ti y en tu visión.

Su perspectiva puede brindarle un impulso muy necesario cuando su confianza flaquea. A veces, simplemente escuchar una perspectiva externa puede reafirmar tu fe en ti mismo.

CÓMO TE VE FORMA TU REALIDAD, LO QUE CREES LO LOGRAS, CÓMO ACTÚAS LO TRANSFORMAS.

"

Practicar el diálogo interno positivo es otra estrategia clave. Reemplace los pensamientos críticos o dudosos con afirmaciones de su fuerza y capacidad. Frases como "Soy capaz", "He superado desafíos antes y puedo volver a hacerlo" pueden ser motivadores poderosos. Recuerde, la forma en que se habla a sí mismo es sumamente importante.

También puede ser útil establecer objetivos realistas y dividirlos en tareas manejables. Cada tarea completada es una pequeña victoria, un paso adelante y un pilar para su confianza. Se trata de crear un ciclo de refuerzo positivo, donde cada pequeño éxito alimenta tu confianza en ti mismo.

Aceptar el aprendizaje y el crecimiento es esencial. Considere los desafíos no como obstáculos insuperables sino como oportunidades para aprender y mejorar. Con cada nueva habilidad que adquieres y cada conocimiento que adquieres, las dudas sobre ti mismo son reemplazadas por una sensación de logro y crecimiento.

Finalmente, sé amable contigo mismo. El emprendimiento es un viaje con sus altibajos. Trátese a sí mismo con la misma compasión y aliento que le ofrecería a un querido amigo. La autocompasión no se trata sólo de ser amable; se trata de ser realista y comprensivo contigo mismo, reconociendo que el camino hacia el éxito es un proceso de aprendizaje.

Superar las dudas sobre uno mismo no se trata de no sentirlas nunca; se trata de no dejar que controle tus decisiones y defina tu viaje. Se trata de reconocer tus miedos pero elegir centrarte en tus fortalezas y potencial. Al pasar la página de las dudas, se abre un capítulo en el que usted es el arquitecto capaz y confiado de su propio éxito. Demos un paso adelante con un renovado sentido de confianza en nosotros mismos, listos para afrontar el mundo del emprendimiento con confianza y determinación.

08 CAPÍTULO OCHO

SUPERAR EL MIEDO AL FRACASO

A medida que nos adentramos más en el ámbito del emprendimiento, nos encontramos con dos enemigos formidables: el miedo al fracaso y el síndrome del impostor. Estos desafíos, si no se controlan, pueden obstaculizar nuestro progreso. Sin embargo, cuando se los confronta y los supera, se convierten en puntos fundamentales de crecimiento y autorrealización.

El miedo al fracaso es como una sombra que acompaña a todo emprendimiento. Es el "qué pasaría si" lo que permanece en el fondo de tu mente. Pero ¿qué pasa si replanteamos el fracaso? En lugar de verlo como una derrota, considérelo como un maestro. Cada fracaso está lleno de lecciones y conocimientos que pueden perfeccionar sus estrategias y fortalecer su determinación. Acepta el fracaso como un paso natural en el proceso empresarial, un paso que te acerca al éxito.

El síndrome del impostor, por otro lado, es el sentimiento de que no perteneces o no mereces tus logros. Es una experiencia común, especialmente cuando se aventura en nuevos territorios. La clave para superar el síndrome del impostor radica en reconocer su valor y sus logros. Entiende que ser emprendedor no significa saberlo todo. Se trata de aprendizaje, crecimiento y adaptación continuos.

Desarrollar la resiliencia contra el miedo al fracaso comienza con el establecimiento de expectativas realistas. No todos los esfuerzos serán un éxito rotundo y eso está bien. Es importante establecer metas que lo desafíen pero que sean alcanzables. Este equilibrio reduce la presión y le permite abordar las tareas con una mente más clara y concentrada.

Enfrentar el síndrome del impostor implica reconocer y celebrar sus éxitos. Mantenga un registro de sus logros, comentarios e hitos. Revíselos cuando surjan dudas. Recuerde, se ha ganado su lugar gracias al trabajo duro, la dedicación y el talento. No eres un impostor; eres un pionero.

Compartir sus miedos y dudas con compañeros o mentores de confianza puede ser una estrategia increíblemente eficaz. Hablar abiertamente sobre sus desafíos a menudo revela que otros han recorrido caminos similares y enfrentaron obstáculos similares. Esta experiencia compartida puede ser inmensamente validadora y reconfortante, recordándote que no estás solo en tu viaje. La fortaleza que se encuentra en estas experiencias compartidas puede ser una poderosa fuente de apoyo e inspiración, fomentando un sentido de comunidad y resiliencia.

Practicar la autocompasión también es vital. Afronte los contratiempos con gentileza y comprensión. Reconozca que luchar por la perfección puede ser una búsqueda interminable y que cada emprendedor, sin importar cuán exitoso sea, enfrenta sus propios obstáculos. La diferencia clave está en cómo maneja y crece a partir de estos desafíos. Trátese a sí mismo con la misma amabilidad, paciencia y empatía que le brindaría a un amigo cercano. Esta autocompasión no es un signo de debilidad, sino un aspecto fundamental para desarrollar la resiliencia y mantener el bienestar en su camino empresarial.

Además, la práctica de visualizar su éxito puede ser transformadora. Tómate el tiempo para imaginar vívidamente superando tus miedos y logrando tus objetivos. Imagínese triunfando en sus esfuerzos, superando obstáculos y alcanzando sus metas. La visualización no es sólo soñar despierto; Es un poderoso ejercicio mental que puede reforzar tu confianza en ti mismo, aumentar tu confianza y motivarte a superar incluso los desafíos más difíciles. Al visualizar periódicamente su éxito, puede crear un plan mental sólido que guíe sus acciones y decisiones hacia el logro de sus objetivos.

El punto nunca fue que ajustaras todo lo que te rodea hasta que fuera perfecto, sino que ajustaras la forma en que ves todo hasta que te des cuenta de que es suficiente, y siempre lo ha sido.
BriannaWiest

AUTO – SABOTAJE

Este capítulo, si bien se centra en transformar la duda en uno mismo, se alinea maravillosamente con las enseñanzas que se encuentran en el libro de Brianna Wiest, "La montaña eres tú". El trabajo de Wiest profundiza en el concepto de autosabotaje y en cómo nuestros propios pensamientos y creencias a menudo pueden ser los mayores obstáculos a los que nos enfrentamos.

Así como exploramos la importancia de reconocer la duda como una respuesta normal al crecimiento y al cambio, Wiest enfatiza la necesidad de comprender y desmantelar los comportamientos y pensamientos de autosabotaje que nos frenan. Su enfoque para superar estos desafíos internos complementa nuestras estrategias para generar confianza y resiliencia en el mundo empresarial.

En "La montaña eres tú", Wiest fomenta una introspección profunda para comprender las causas fundamentales de nuestras dudas y miedos. De manera similar, en este capítulo enfatizamos la importancia de reconocer sus logros y utilizar el diálogo interno positivo como herramientas para combatir las dudas. La noción de Wiest de reescribir nuestra narrativa y cambiar la forma en que nos hablamos a nosotros mismos refleja nuestro énfasis en reemplazar los pensamientos críticos con afirmaciones de fuerza y capacidad.

Además, el libro de Wiest subraya el poder de asumir la responsabilidad de nuestro viaje y la transformación que se produce cuando dejamos de vernos a nosotros mismos como víctimas de las circunstancias. Esto se alinea con nuestro estímulo para ver los desafíos no como obstáculos insuperables sino como oportunidades de aprendizaje y crecimiento.

Incorporar la sabiduría de "La montaña eres tú" a tu vida proporciona una capa adicional de comprensión y estrategia para superar las dudas. Las ideas de Wiest pueden actuar como una guía para ayudarle a usted, el emprendedor, a reconocer que el viaje hacia la confianza en uno mismo tiene que ver tanto con la transformación interna como con el logro externo.

Supere las dudas sobre uno mismo:

- Busque crecimiento, no sólo validación.
- Apunte a la excelencia personal, no solo a ser el primero o el mejor.
- Celebre el progreso personal, no sólo la aclamación pública.
- Abrace su viaje único, no solo el destino.
- Busque la realización personal, no sólo la aprobación externa.
- Valorar el autodescubrimiento por encima de las expectativas sociales

Al combinar nuestros pasos prácticos con los profundos conocimientos del trabajo de Wiest, estará equipado no sólo para pasar la página de las dudas, sino también para reescribir toda su historia. Abrace este viaje de transformación, donde cada paso adelante remodela su narrativa con fuerza y propósito. Deje que esta combinación de sabiduría sea su guía a medida que avanza con confianza renovada, listo para enfrentarse al mundo empresarial con un fuerte sentido de confianza en sí mismo y determinación.

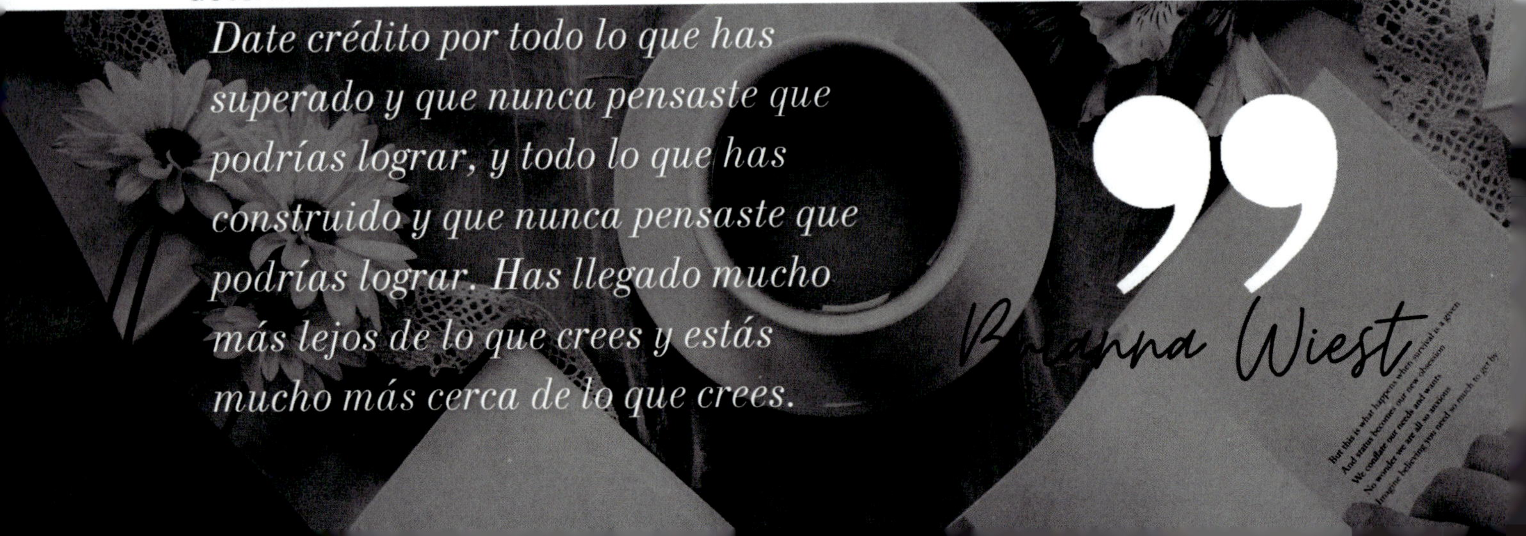

Date crédito por todo lo que has superado y que nunca pensaste que podrías lograr, y todo lo que has construido y que nunca pensaste que podrías lograr. Has llegado mucho más lejos de lo que crees y estás mucho más cerca de lo que crees.

Brianna Wiest

09

CAPÍTULO NUEVE

LIBERARSE DEL PERFECCIONISMO

Recordatorio de hoy

No dejes que
el enemigo de
la perfección ser
el del progreso

LEYENDO LIBRE DE PERFECCIONISMO

En nuestro camino como emprendedores, la lucha por la excelencia es encomiable, pero cuando se transforma en perfeccionismo, se convierte en una barrera para el progreso y la creatividad. El perfeccionismo, la búsqueda incesante de la perfección, puede sofocar el crecimiento, obstaculi-zar la productividad y agotar la energía. Este capítulo está dedicado a liberarse de las cadenas del perfeccionismo y aceptar la imperfección como un camino hacia el éxito y la innovación.

Comprender la naturaleza del perfeccionismo es el primer paso. A menudo surge del miedo al juicio o al fracaso, lo que lleva a analizar demasiado y obsesionarse con los detalles. Pero en el dinámico mundo de los negocios, la flexibilidad y la adaptabilidad son claves. El perfeccionismo puede limitar estas cualidades, dificultando la toma de decisiones o la asunción de riesgos.

Reconocer los signos de perfeccionismo en sus hábitos laborales es fundamental. ¿Dedica dema-siado tiempo a las tareas por temor a que no sean "perfectas"? ¿Dudas en lanzar un producto o servicio porque no es perfecto a tus ojos? Estas son señales reveladoras de que el perfeccionismo podría estar frenándote.

EL ÉXITO ES SU VIAJE, NO EL DESTINO.

Aquí hay algunas estrategias que personalmente he encontrado efectivas para superar la tentación del perfeccionismo, un desafío al que me he enfrentado yo mismo. Espero que estas ideas, extraídas de mi propio viaje, puedan ofrecerles una guía práctica y un sentido de solidaridad mientras superan este obstáculo común.

1 *Establecer estándares y objetivos realistas*

Este enfoque consiste en alinear sus expectativas con lo que es alcanzable y manejable, considerando los recursos y el tiempo que tiene. Se trata de definir el éxito de una manera que sea alcanzable y deje espacio para el flujo y reflujo natural del proceso empresarial. Reconozca que luchar por la excelencia es un viaje y que la perfección no es un destino realista o necesario.

Establecer objetivos realistas también implica valorar el proceso de crecimiento de tu negocio. Es comprender que cada paso adelante, sea perfecto o no, es parte de tu progreso. Esta mentalidad ayuda a desarrollar la resiliencia frente a los reveses que son una parte inherente de cualquier viaje empresarial. Además, le permite celebrar las pequeñas victorias y el progreso incremental, que a menudo quedan eclipsados por la búsqueda de un ideal inalcanzable., que a menudo quedan eclipsados

2 *La filosofía "suficientemente buena"*

De hecho, adoptar una filosofía "suficientemente buena" puede resultar liberador. Se trata de comprender el equilibrio entre perfección y practicidad. Este enfoque no se trata de rebajar los estándares, sino de reconocer cuándo una tarea logra su propósito sin refinarla demasiado.

Un resultado "suficientemente bueno" es a menudo lo que impulsa el progreso, permitiéndole avanzar, experimentar con nuevos conceptos y recopilar comentarios valiosos. Esta mentalidad ayuda a mantener el impulso y la eficiencia, garantizando un progreso continuo sin quedarse estancado en la búsqueda de una perfección inalcanzable.

3 *Establecer plazos*

Los plazos actúan como una lente de enfoque, guiándote a concentrarte en lo que realmente importa y evitando perderte en los detalles. Esta práctica ayuda a priorizar las tareas y gestionar el tiempo, mejorando tanto la productividad como la eficiencia.

Al cumplir con los plazos, se crea un enfoque estructurado que agiliza los procesos, asegurando que la energía y los recursos se dirijan hacia el logro de objetivos clave dentro de un plazo específico. Esto no sólo ayuda a mantener un ritmo constante de trabajo sino también a lograr un mayor nivel de organización y claridad en sus operaciones comerciales.

4 *Renuncia a la necesidad de hacerlo todo tú mismo*

Delegar tareas también puede ayudar a superar el perfeccionismo. Confía en tu equipo para encargarse de determinadas tareas. Esto no sólo alivia su carga de trabajo, sino que también ayuda a crear un entorno de equipo colaborativo y de confianza. La delegación te enseña que el control no siempre es la clave del éxito; A veces se trata de dejarse llevar.

5 *Cultivar una mentalidad de crecimiento*

En lugar de aspirar a la perfección, concéntrese en lograr avances y mejoras constantes. Celebre cada avance, sin importar su tamaño, y reconozca que el camino empresarial es uno de aprendizaje y evolución continuos. Este cambio de mentalidad de la perfección al progreso no sólo alivia la presión indebida sino que también fomenta un enfoque más adaptable e innovador a los desafíos empresariales, haciendo que el viaje en sí sea tan gratificante como el destino.

EL ÉXITO ES GUSTARTE A TI MISMO, QUE TE GUSTE LO QUE HACES Y QUE TE GUSTE CÓMO LO HACES.

Acepta tus *Imperfecciones!*

Basándonos en nuestra comprensión de cómo liberarnos del perfeccionismo, inspirémonos en "Los dones de la imperfección" de Brené Brown. El perspicaz trabajo de Brown arroja luz sobre cómo aceptar nuestras vulnerabilidades e imperfecciones es crucial para llevar una vida incon-dicional, una lección que es increíblemente relevante para el viaje empresarial.

Brown enfatiza la idea de una "vida incondicional", un proceso de involucrarnos en nuestras vidas desde un lugar de dignidad. Se trata de cultivar el coraje, la compasión y la conexión para despertarnos por la mañana y pensar: "No importa lo que se haga y lo que quede por hacer, soy suficiente". Esta filosofía es un poderoso antídoto contra el perfeccionismo que a menudo afecta a los empresarios.

En el contexto de los negocios, aceptar sus imperfecciones significa reconocer que no todas las empresas, productos o decisiones serán impecables, y eso está bien. Se trata de encontrar el coraje para ser vulnerable, para asumir riesgos incluso cuando no hay garantía de éxito. Brown nos anima a ver la vulnerabilidad no como una debilidad, sino como una fortaleza.

Una de las enseñanzas clave de Brown es la importancia de la autocompasión. Como empren-dedores, ser amables con nosotros mismos, especialmente cuando tropezamos, es vital. La autocompasión nos permite ver los errores no como fracasos, sino como oportunidades de crecimiento y aprendizaje. Se trata de aceptar la idea de que lo que nos hace vulnerables también nos hace hermosos.

Cuanto más intentas complacer a todos, más te alejas de tu esencia única.

Además, Brown analiza el poder de dejar de lado lo que la gente piensa. En los negocios, esto se traduce en centrarse en su visión y sus valores, en lugar de quedar atrapado en tratar de complacer a todos o cumplir con estándares externos de perfección. Se trata de tener el coraje de ser auténtico y fiel a tu visión, incluso si va contra la corriente.

Liberarse del perfeccionismo no es un proceso de la noche a la mañana y no se trata sólo de cambiar hábitos, sino también de una transformación más profunda de la mentalidad. Se trata de aceptar la imperfección como una parte natural y necesaria del crecimiento y la innovación. A medida que avanzamos, recordemos que en el panorama empresarial en constante evolución, la flexibilidad, la adaptabilidad y la me-jora continua son las verdaderas características del éxito. Acojamos la imperfección como nuestra aliada, abriendo las puertas a nuevas posibilidades y oportunidades.

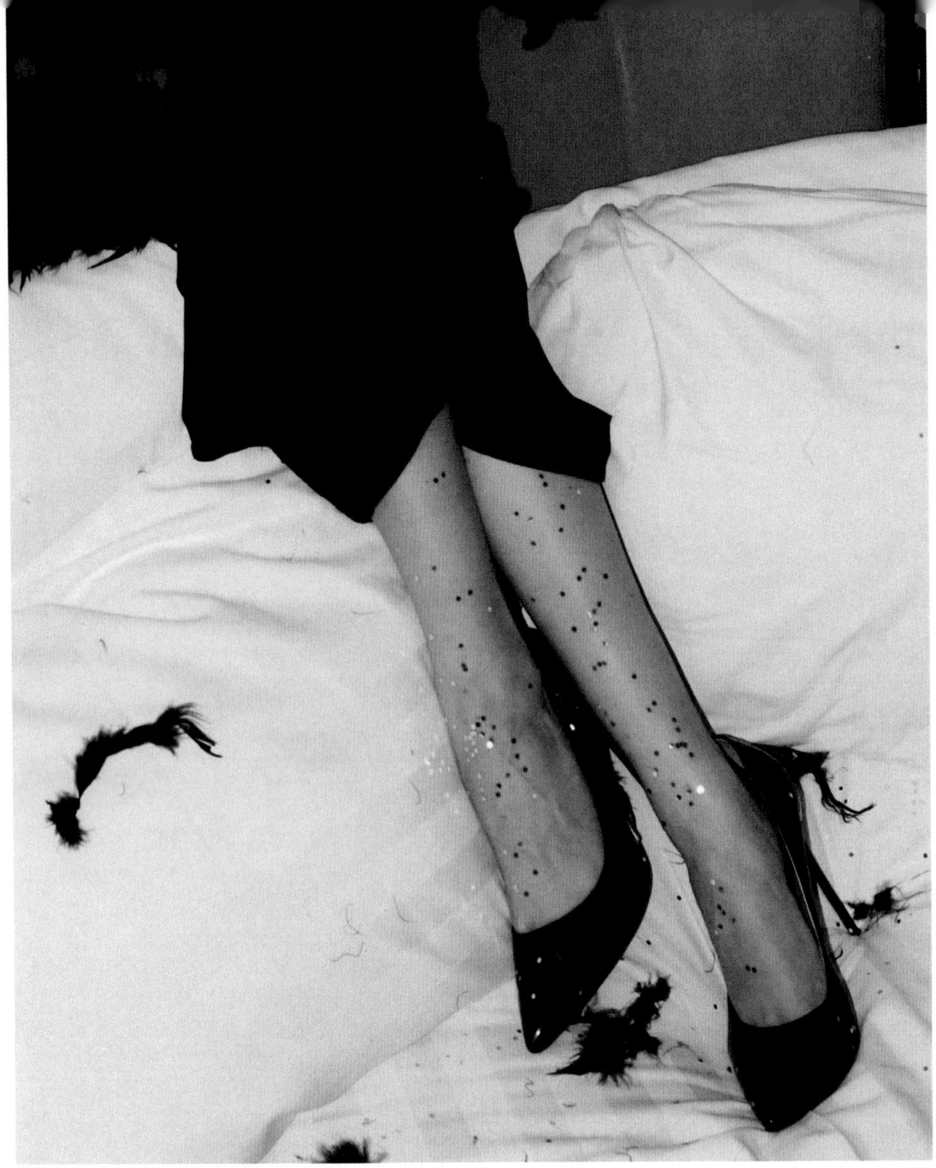

Comprender la diferencia entre el esfuerzo saludable y el perfeccionismo es fundamental para dejar el escudo y retomar la vida. Las investigaciones muestran que el perfeccionismo obstaculiza el éxito. De hecho, suele ser el camino hacia la depresión, la ansiedad, la adicción y la parálisis de la vida

Brene Brown

CAPÍTULO DIEZ

DE LA COMPARACIÓN A LA INSPIRACIÓN

DE COMPARACIÓN A *Inspiración*

En nuestro viaje empresarial, es natural mirar a nuestro alrededor y comparar nuestro progreso con el de otros. Sin embargo, esta comparación a menudo puede generar dudas y un sentimiento de insuficiencia. Este capítulo trata de cambiar esa perspectiva

de la comparación a la inspiración, transformando la forma en que vemos los éxitos de los demás y utilizándolos para impulsar nuestro crecimiento.

En el mundo empresarial, es fácil caer en la trampa de comparar su comienzo con el desarrollo de otra persona. Recuerde, algunas de las personas con las que podría compararse podrían haber comenzado su trayectoria empresarial mucho antes y podrían estar en una etapa más avanzada. Esta comparación no sólo es injusta; puede distorsionar su percepción de sus logros y progreso.

Más bien, transformemos la comparación en una fuente de inspiración. Cuando veas que alguien logra el éxito, úsalo como motivación. Analiza qué hicieron bien y cómo puedes incorporar estrategias o ideas similares en tu negocio. Se trata de aprender de los éxitos de los demás y convertir la admiración en conocimientos prácticos.

Celebrar los éxitos de los demás también es un poderoso cambio de mentalidad. Cuando apreciamos y aplaudimos los logros de nuestros pares, se crea un ambiente positivo, tanto internamente como dentro de su red comercial. Esta positividad no solo es edificante; Fomenta una comunidad de apoyo y colaboración.

CONCENTRARSE EN

Ti mismo

Otro aspecto importante es centrarse en su viaje y sus hitos. Cada empresa y emprendedor tiene un camino único con diferentes desafíos y oportunidades. Concéntrate en tus objeti-vos, tu progreso y lo lejos que has llegado. Este enfoque propio minimiza el impacto de la comparación y lo mantiene alineado con su visión.

Participar en la autorreflexión es una forma constructiva de lidiar con los sentimientos de comparación. Reflexiona sobre tus valores, tu misión y tu definición de éxito. Esta intros-pección te fundamenta y te recuerda que tu viaje consiste en cumplir tu visión única, no en emular el camino de otra persona.

TU VIAJE, TUS HITOS

Buscar historias de luchas y fracasos detrás de los éxitos de otros es una experiencia esclarecedora. Pinta una imagen más completa y realista del viaje hacia el éxito, enfatizando que no es un camino recto sino un camino sinuoso lleno de oportunidades de aprendizaje, crecimiento y perseverancia para superar los desafíos. Esta comprensión es crucial para darse cuenta de que el verdadero éxito a menudo proviene de resistir tiempos difíciles y salir más fuerte.

Además, rodearse de una amplia gama de modelos a seguir y fuentes de inspiración es invaluable. Al interactuar con personas de diversas industrias, orígenes y etapas de su trayectoria empresarial, obtendrá una perspectiva más amplia e inclusiva sobre cómo puede ser el éxito. Esta diversidad resalta que el éxito no es monolítico sino variado y único para cada individuo. Recuerde, la comparación más significativa es consigo mismo.

Concéntrate en tu crecimiento personal, celebra tus propios hitos y reconoce que cada pequeño logro es un paso adelante en tu camino único.

Al centrar su atención en su viaje personal y obtener motivación de un amplio espectro de historias de éxito, puede utilizar eficazmente la comparación como herramienta de crecimiento e inspiración.

Este cambio empoderador y de mentalidad es lo ienta a ver su viaje empresarial a través de una lente de ositividad y superación personal.

Tu única competencia erdadera es la persona que eras ayer. Esfuércese por uperar su pasado, no el de los demás.

CELEBRE SU VIAJE

11 CAPÍTULO ONCE

CONSTRUYENDO UNA HERMANDAD SOLIDARIA EN LOS NEGOCIOS

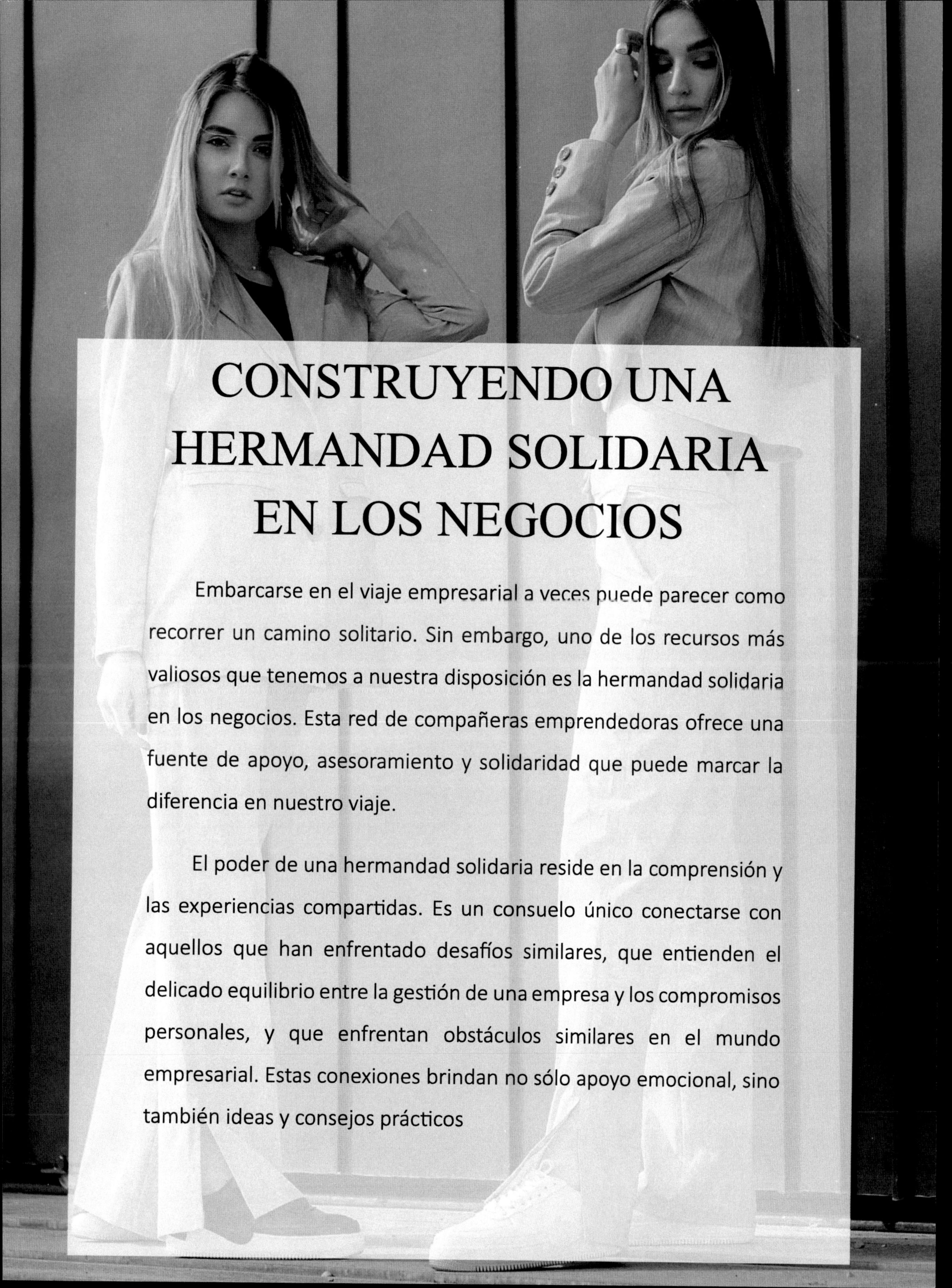

CONSTRUYENDO UNA HERMANDAD SOLIDARIA EN LOS NEGOCIOS

Embarcarse en el viaje empresarial a veces puede parecer como recorrer un camino solitario. Sin embargo, uno de los recursos más valiosos que tenemos a nuestra disposición es la hermandad solidaria en los negocios. Esta red de compañeras emprendedoras ofrece una fuente de apoyo, asesoramiento y solidaridad que puede marcar la diferencia en nuestro viaje.

El poder de una hermandad solidaria reside en la comprensión y las experiencias compartidas. Es un consuelo único conectarse con aquellos que han enfrentado desafíos similares, que entienden el delicado equilibrio entre la gestión de una empresa y los compromisos personales, y que enfrentan obstáculos similares en el mundo empresarial. Estas conexiones brindan no sólo apoyo emocional, sino también ideas y consejos prácticos

La colaboración con la hermandad de mujeres empresarias puede adoptar diversas formas y estructuras. Podría implicar unirse a un grupo de networking formal, convertirse en parte de una comunidad en línea o incluso participar en reuniones informales y encuentros de mujeres con ideas afines. Cada una de estas plataformas ofrece sus propios beneficios y oportunidades de conexión únicos.

El aspecto crucial es encontrar un espacio donde te sientas cómodo para compartir abiertamente tus experiencias, absorber nuevos conocimientos y desarrollarte tanto personal como profesionalmente.

Dentro de estos grupos, descubrirá una rica reserva de sabiduría y experiencia.

Desde complejas estrategias de marketing hasta consejos prácticos sobre financiación, los conocimientos disponibles a menudo se ven moldeados y enriquecidos por la experiencia colectiva de ser mujer en el mundo empresarial.

Este entorno de aprendizaje comunitario fomenta no sólo el crecimiento profesional sino también un sentido de solidaridad y apoyo, lo cual es invaluable en el viaje empresarial.

La colaboración es otro hermoso aspecto de la hermandad. Se trata de reconocer que no tenemos por qué competir unos con otros. En cambio, podemos aunar nuestras habilidades, recursos y redes para crear oportunidades que beneficien a todos los involucrados. Las colaboraciones pueden abrir nuevos mercados, ampliar las bases de clientes y aportar nuevas ideas y perspectivas a nuestros negocios.

Las mujeres empoderan a las mujeres

La tutoría dentro de la hermandad es igualmente valiosa. Ya sea usted un mentor o un aprendiz, estas relaciones pueden ser increíblemente gratificantes.

Son una oportunidad para el crecimiento personal y para retribuir, compartiendo tus experiencias y lecciones con aquellos que están donde tú alguna vez estuviste.

Ser mentor también puede proporcionar nuevos conocimientos sobre su propio negocio, viendo las cosas desde una perspectiva nueva.

REMANDO JUNTOS

Celebrar los éxitos de cada una es la piedra angular de esta hermandad. En un mundo que a menudo enfrenta a las mujeres entre sí, elegir celebrar y animarse mutuamente es una declaración poderosa. Crea un ambiente de respeto y admiración mutuos, donde se comparten los éxitos y se multiplican los logros.

Lo más importante es que la hermandad proporciona un sentido de pertenencia. Es un recordatorio de que no estás solo en este viaje. Hay otros que comparten tus sueños, tus luchas y tus aspiraciones. Este sentido de comunidad no sólo es reconfortante; es empoderador. Refuerza su coraje, fortalece su determinación y enriquece su experiencia empresarial.

12

CAPÍTULO DOCE

CREAR UNA VISIÓN PERSONAL DEL ÉXITO

SU VISIÓN DE ÉXITO

El éxito, a menudo visto como un destino único para todos, es en realidad profundamente personal y único. Este capítulo trata sobre cómo descubrir lo que real-mente significa el éxito para usted y cómo utilizar técnicas de visualización para hacer realidad sus objetivos y aspiraciones comerciales.

El éxito en los negocios se mide tradicionalmente mediante métricas financieras, pero cuando hablamos de una visión personal del éxito, abarca mucho más. Se trata de alinear los logros de su negocio con sus valores, deseos y objetivos de vi-da personales. Podría significar tener la flexibilidad de pasar más tiempo con la familia, generar un impacto significativo en su comunidad o lograr una sensación de realización personal y felicidad.

Empiece por reflexionar sobre lo que le hace sentir realizado y contento. ¿Es la cantidad de ventas que realiza, los comentarios de clientes satisfechos, el estilo de vida que le brinda su empresa o el crecimiento y desarrollo de su equipo? Com-prender estos elementos ayuda a dar forma a una visión de éxito que resuena con usted en un nivel más profundo.

LA VISUALIZACIÓN ES UNA HERRAMIENTA PODEROSA EN ESTE PROCESO

Implica crear una imagen mental del resultado deseado, imaginando no sólo el objetivo final sino también los pasos y los hitos a lo largo del camino. Esta práctica no sólo aclara tu visión sino que también la incrusta en tu subconsciente, alineando tus pensamientos y acciones con tus objetivos.

Para utilizar la visualización de forma eficaz, busque un espacio y un momento tranquilos donde pueda concentrarse sin interrupciones. Cierra los ojos e imagina alcanzar tu versión del éxito. Visualiza los sentimientos, el entorno, las personas que te rodean. Cuanto más detallada y vívida sea tu visualización, más impactante será.

Incorpora esta práctica a tu rutina. La visualización constante refuerza tus objetivos y te mantiene motivado, especialmente en tiempos difíciles. Es un recordatorio de hacia qué estás trabajando y por qué es importante.

LA TÉCNICA DE VISUALIZACIÓN DE LAS "MAÑANAS MILAGROSAS"

Hal Elrod, en su libro "The Miracle Morning", no sólo profundiza en el concepto de visualización sino que también enfatiza su profundo impacto. Describe tres pasos sencillos para integrar perfectamente la visualización creativa en tu ritual matutino. Además, Elrod explica cómo un tablero de visión puede ser una herramienta potente en su camino hacia el éxito.

En el ámbito de Miracle Morning, la visualización se entrelaza perfectamente con la práctica de afirmaciones para programar su mente subconsciente para el triunfo. Si bien algunos pueden atribuirlo a la "ley de la atracción", es innegable que la visualización conlleva beneficios tangibles.

Adopte la rutina de visualización de Mañanas Milagrosas con estos tres sencillos pasos, inmediatamente después de su práctica de afirmación:

Preparar el escenario

Cree una atmósfera serena, quizás acompañada de música instrumental suave como la de Bach tocando suavemente de fondo. Siéntese cómodamente, con la columna erguida y respire profundamente y limpiando. Cierra los ojos y vacía tu mente, preparándola para el vívido viaje mental que te espera.

Visualice los resultados deseados

Sumérgete profundamente en tus sueños durante esta visualización de Mañanas Milagrosas. Involucre sus sentidos para ver, oír, sentir, tocar, oler y saborear vívidamente cada faceta de sus aspiraciones. Cuanto más intrincado y realista sea tu cuadro mental, más avivará el fuego de la motivación en tu interior. Visualízate no sólo logrando tus objetivos, sino también saboreando la satisfacción de haberlos cumplido.

Encarna tu yo ideal

Una vez que tengas una idea clara de adónde quieres ir, imagina que eres el tipo de persona que puede llegar allí. Imagínate haciendo las cosas que necesitas hacer, como estudiar, escribir, hacer llamadas importantes o lo que sea necesario para alcanzar tu objetivo. Imagínese luciendo confiado y decidido.

PODER DE LAS AFIRMACIONES

Las afirmaciones son como mantras poderosos que pueden remodelar su forma de pensar y allanar el camino hacia el éxito. Estas declaraciones concisas pero impactantes sirven como recordatorios de sus metas, valores y aspiraciones.

Al repetir afirmaciones con convicción, refuerzas las creencias positivas y fortaleces tu confianza en ti mismo. En este viaje de superación personal, las afirmaciones actúan como luces guía, ayudándote a mantenerte concentrado, motivado y alineado con tus verdaderos deseos. Entonces, embarquémonos en este viaje transformador a través del mundo de las afirmaciones, donde exploraremos su significado y descubriremos cómo pueden empoderarlo en su búsqueda de crecimiento personal y profesional.

- Soy una mujer fuerte y resiliente, capaz de superar cualquier reto. Cada día, en todos los sentidos, tengo más confianza y éxito.

- Los desafíos son oportunidades para crecer y aprender.

- Soy una mujer exitosa, logro mis objetivos e inspiro a otros con mi viaje. Confío en mi intuición y tomo decisiones con claridad y confianza. Soy concentrado, persistente y nunca me rendiré.

- Soy capaz de lograr grandes cosas.

- Soy merecedor de mis sueños y trabajo por ellos todos los días. Soy digno del éxito y la prosperidad.

- Acepto el cambio y me adapto a nuevas situaciones con facilidad. Creo la vida que deseo con confianza y entusiasmo.

- Los obstáculos son simplemente peldaños en mi camino hacia el éxito. Mi arduo trabajo y dedicación me traerán el éxito.

- El éxito es un viaje, no un destino, y disfruto cada paso. Soy un imán para las oportunidades positivas y el éxito. Soy resiliente, fuerte y valiente ante los desafíos.

- Con cada respiración, libero dudas y doy la bienvenida a la confianza. Confío en mi intuición y tomo decisiones con claridad y confianza. Abrazo a mi jefe interior, nena, liderando con confianza y determinación. Mi potencial para tener éxito es ilimitado.

TABLERO DE VISION

Para mejorar aún más su viaje de visualización, considere crear un tablero de visión como ayuda adicional. Esta obra maestra visual sirve como una representación tangible de sus aspiraciones, incorporando imágenes, citas e inspiraciones que personifican el futuro deseado. Si bien mirar su tablero de visión puede ser inspirador y ayudar a mantener la concentración, recuerde que tomar acciones concretas sigue siendo la piedra angular para transformar sus sueños en realidad.

Recuerde ser flexible con su visión. A medida que crezca y evolucione, también lo hará su definición de éxito. Revise y revise su visión según sea necesario, adaptándola a nuevos aprendizajes y experiencias. Esta flexibilidad no es un signo de indecisión sino de crecimiento y madurez como emprendedor.

Por último, celebre cada paso hacia su visión. Reconoce los pequeños logros en el camino. Estas celebraciones refuerzan tu progreso y te mantienen lleno de energía y concentrado en el viaje que tienes por delante.

Al crear y visualizar su visión personal del éxito, no sólo está estableciendo metas; estás alineando tus valores y aspiraciones más profundos con tu camino empresarial. Esta alineación aporta una sensación de propósito y satisfacción que trasciende las medidas convencionales de éxito. Al cerrar este capítulo, llevemos adelante esta visión, usándola como luz guía en nuestro viaje empresarial, iluminando nuestro camino con claridad, propósito y realización

TIENES EL VALOR DE EMPEZAR DE NUEVO...
AHORA REPITE...

CONCLUSIÓN

Al cerrar las páginas de "Mentalidad de la mujer emprendedora para el éxito", tómate un momento para apreciar el viaje que hemos compartido. Desde descubrir su "por qué" en los negocios hasta crear su visión personal del éxito, cada capítulo ha sido un paso para empoderarla como mujer emprendedora. Hemos abordado temas cruciales como convertir la pasión en ganancias, abrazar la intuición y superar las dudas, equipándote con las herramientas para prosperar en tu viaje empresarial.

Ahora, mientras estás en esta coyuntura, armado con conocimientos e ideas, recuerda que el verdadero poder está dentro de ti. Eres capaz, resiliente y estás preparado para el éxito. Deje que las lecciones aprendidas sean su guía, pero confíe en sus instintos y su visión única a medida que avanza. Usted puede moldear su camino empresarial, lleno de posibilidades, aprendizaje y triunfos.

Abrace su viaje con audacia y confianza. Los desafíos que enfrentas son simplemente oportunidades para mostrar tu fuerza y creatividad. Celebre cada logro, aprenda de cada revés y siga superando los límites de lo que puede lograr. No sólo estás construyendo un negocio; estás creando un legado.

Manténgase conectado con su hermandad, obtenga fuerzas de su comunidad y continúe siendo un faro de inspiración para otros. Su historia es de empoderamiento, resiliencia y éxito. Sigue brillando, sigue esforzándote y recuerda: tú eres el arquitecto de tu destino. Por su éxito continuo y el extraordinario viaje que le espera como mujer emprendedora.

13 CAPÍTULO TRECE

CÓMO LANZAR TU NEGOCIO DIGITAL EN 30 DÍAS

Día 1 - 5: Sentar las bases

Identificar y especializarse en un nicho dentro del ámbito del marketing digital es crucial para destacar en un mercado competitivo. Su nicho podría basarse en la

industria (p. ej., marketing digital para atención médica o educación), servicio (p. ej., SEO, marketing en redes sociales, marketing por correo electrónico) o incluso un tipo particular de cliente (p. ej., empresas emergentes, empresas locales, comercio electrónico).

1. COMPRENDER SU NICHO

Investigación: realice una investigación de mercado exhaustiva para comprender dónde se cruzan su pasión y sus habilidades con las necesidades del mercado. Herramientas como Google Trends, informes de la industria y análisis de la competencia pueden ofrecer información valiosa.

Defina su cliente ideal: visualice a su cliente perfecto: su industria, tamaño, desafíos y objetivos. Esta claridad guiará su desarrollo de marketing y servicios.

Evalúe la competencia: observe otras empresas en el nicho de mercado que propone. Identifique los vacíos en sus ofertas que pueda llenar.

2. ELABORACIÓN DE SU PLAN DE NEGOCIOS

- Un plan de negocios es su hoja de ruta, que describe sus objetivos y estrategias comerciales y cómo planea lograrlos. También es esencial para asegurar inversiones o préstamos.

- Resumen ejecutivo: comience con un resumen claro y conciso de su idea de negocio, incluido el nombre de su empresa, los servicios que ofrecerá y su mercado objetivo.

- Objetivos comerciales: enumere sus metas a corto y largo plazo. Sea específico sobre lo que quiere lograr durante el primer año.
- Análisis de mercado: detalle los resultados de su investigación sobre su nicho, mercado objetivo y competencia. Destacar tendencias y necesidades de los clientes.
- Servicios y Precios: Defina los servicios de marketing digital que ofrecerá. Incluya modelos o rangos de precios basados en su investigación de mercado.
- Estrategia de marketing y ventas: describa cómo atraerá y retendrá clientes. Incluya tácticas de marketing tanto online como offline.
- Plan financiero: proyecte sus costos iniciales, estrategia de precios, proyecciones de ingresos y cronograma de rentabilidad. Se pueden utilizar herramientas como Excel o Google Sheets para realizar modelos financieros.
- Plan operativo: describa el flujo de trabajo operativo de su empresa, incluidos los procesos de adquisición de clientes, gestión de proyectos y entrega.

Los primeros cinco días tratan de establecer una base sólida para su negocio de marketing digital. Al comprender su nicho de mercado y elaborar un plan de negocios detallado, estará sentando las bases para un lanzamiento enfocado y exitoso. Recuerde, la clave para una base sólida es una investigación exhaustiva, una planificación clara y un pensamiento estratégico.

TIPS PARA *éxito*

- SEA FLEXIBLE: SU PLAN DE NEGOCIOS NO ESTÁ ESCRITO EN PIEDRA. ESTÉ PREPARADO PARA ADAPTARLO A MEDIDA QUE APRENDA MÁS SOBRE SU MERCADO Y SUS CLIENTES.

- CONCÉNTRESE EN SU PROPUESTA DE VENTA ÚNICA (PVU): ARTICULE CLARAMENTE QUÉ HACE QUE SU NEGOCIO DE MARKETING DIGITAL SEA DIFERENTE Y MEJOR PARA SUS CLIENTES OBJETIVO.

- BUSQUE COMENTARIOS: COMPARTA SU PLAN DE NEGOCIOS CON MENTORES O ASESORES CONFIABLES Y PERFECCIONELO EN FUNCIÓN DE SUS CONOCIMIENTOS.

Día 6-10: Desarrollo de tu producto

Durante esta fase crítica, la atención se centra en transformar su concepto inicial en un producto digital tangible. Este período es donde tu idea comienza a tomar forma, lo que requiere dedicación, creatividad y planificación estratégica. Aquí le mostramos cómo abordar estos días cruciales.

1. Seleccione sus herramientas y plataforma

- Para libros electrónicos y guías: elija herramientas de escritura y diseño como Google Docs para colaboración y Adobe InDesign para diseño. Canva puede ser una opción fácil de usar para quienes no tienen experiencia en diseño gráfico.
- Para cursos en línea: describa la estructura de su curso. Utilice plataformas como Teachable, Thinkific o Udemy, que ofrecen interfaces fáciles de usar para la creación y gestión de cursos.
- Para plantillas de diseño: Adobe Photoshop e Illustrator son herramientas estándar, pero Canva ofrece una alternativa más accesible para quienes no son diseñadores. Determina los tipos de plantillas que crearás, como gráficos para redes sociales, plantillas de presentación o materiales de marketing.

2. Requisitos legales para la creación de contenido

- Primero el esquema: para cualquier producto digital, comience con un esquema claro. Divida capítulos para libros electrónicos, lecciones para cursos o elementos para plantillas de diseño.
- Producción: comienza a crear tu contenido. Para materiales escritos, céntrese en contenido claro, valioso y atractivo. Para los cursos, comience a grabar videos, asegurando una alta calidad de audio y video. Para las plantillas de diseño, cree diseños diversos y visualmente atractivos.
- Garantía de calidad: revise periódicamente la calidad y coherencia de su trabajo. Es útil alejarse y regresar con ojos nuevos o incluso recibir comentarios de sus compañeros.

1. Elija un nombre de dominio y hosting

- Seleccione un nombre de dominio que refleje su marca y sea fácil de recordar. Utilice servicios de alojamiento que sean confiables y escalables, como Bluehost o SiteGround, y considere plataformas CMS como WordPress para obtener flexibilidad en diseño y funcionalidad.

2. Construyendo su sitio web

- Integración de comercio electrónico: utilice WooCommerce para WordPress o elija una plataforma todo en uno como Shopify para vender sus productos digitales.
- Páginas de productos: diseñe páginas de productos atractivas con descripciones claras, imágenes o vistas previas de alta calidad y un proceso de compra sencillo.
- Páginas de contacto y acerca de: estas páginas ayudan a generar confianza con su audiencia. Comparta su historia en la página Acerca de y facilite que los clientes se comuniquen con usted.

3. Preparación para las ventas

- Configuración de la pasarela de pago: integre pasarelas de pago confiables como PayPal, Stripe o Shopify Payments para manejar las transacciones sin problemas.
- Entrega digital de productos: asegúrese de que exista un sistema automatizado para que los clientes reciban sus productos inmediatamente después de la compra. Esto puede ser a través de enlaces de descarga directa o entrega por correo electrónico.

Los días 6 a 10 consisten en profundizar en el desarrollo de productos y sentar una base sólida para su producto digital. Al concentrarse en crear contenido de alta calidad, establecer una presencia en línea eficiente y prepararse para las ventas, estará preparando el escenario para el lanzamiento exitoso de un producto digital.

TIPS PARA *éxito*

- MANTÉNGASE ORGANIZADO: MANTENGA TODOS SUS ARCHIVOS Y RECURSOS BIEN ORGANIZADOS. UTILICE EL ALMACENAMIENTO EN LA NUBE COMO GOOGLE DRIVE O DROPBOX PARA ACCEDER Y REALIZAR COPIAS DE SEGURIDAD FÁCILMENTE.

- CENTRARSE EN EL VALOR: TENGA SIEMPRE PRESENTE AL USUARIO FINAL. SU PRODUCTO DEBE RESOLVER UN PROBLEMA O SATISFACER UNA NECESIDAD DE SU PÚBLICO OBJETIVO.

- ITERAR Y MEJORAR: NO BUSQUE LA PERFECCIÓN EN SU PRIMER INTENTO. LLEVE SU PRODUCTO A UN BUEN LUGAR, LANCE Y ESTÉ ABIERTO A REALIZAR MEJORAS BASADAS EN LOS COMENTARIOS DE LOS CLIENTES.

Día11-15: Desarrollo de marca y sitio web

Esta fase crucial consiste en definir y perfeccionar lo que ofrecerá su negocio de marketing digital. Implica presentar sus servicios de una manera que sea atractiva para su mercado objetivo, establecer su estrategia de precios y preparar una cartera convincente que muestre sus habilidades y experiencia.

DESARROLLO DE MARCA Y SITIO WEB

1. Crear una identidad de marca memorable

- Identidad visual: diseñe un logotipo y elija combinaciones de colores y fuentes que reflejen la personalidad de su marca y atraigan a su mercado objetivo. Canva puede ser una gran herramienta para crear elementos iniciales de marca.
- Voz de marca: establezca una voz y un mensaje de marca coherentes que resuenen con su público objetivo y reflejen los valores de su marca.

2. Creación de un sitio web profesional

- Sistema de gestión de contenido (CMS): elija un CMS como WordPress, Squarespace o Wix que se adapte a sus necesidades y habilidades técnicas.
- Elementos clave: asegúrese de que su sitio web incluya páginas esenciales como Inicio, Acerca de nosotros, Servicios, Portafolio, Blog e Información de contacto.
- SEO: Optimice su sitio web para los motores de búsqueda desde el principio centrándose en la velocidad del sitio, la capacidad de respuesta móvil y el contenido rico en palabras clave.
- Blog: un blog puede generar tráfico a su sitio, mejorar el SEO y establecer su experiencia en su nicho. Publique periódicamente contenido relevante y valioso que su público objetivo encuentre útil.
- Llamado a la acción (CTA): incluya CTA claros en su sitio web para alentar a los visitantes a comprar sus productos.

Los días 11 al 15 están dedicados a establecer su marca y crear un sitio web que no solo luzca profesional sino que también comunique de manera efectiva el mensaje de su marca y muestre sus productos digitales. Un sitio web bien diseñado y una identidad de marca sólida son cruciales para atraer y retener clientes en el competitivo panorama de los productos digitales.

TIPS PARA *éxito*

- TENGA EN CUENTA A SU PÚBLICO: CADA ASPECTO DE SU MARCA Y SITIO WEB DEBE SATISFACER LAS PREFERENCIAS Y NECESIDADES DE SU PÚBLICO OBJETIVO.

- SEA AUTÉNTICO: DEJE QUE LA PERSONALIDAD ÚNICA DE SU MARCA BRILLE EN SU DISEÑO VISUAL Y CONTENIDO.

- ITERAR EN FUNCIÓN DE LOS COMENTARIOS: DESPUÉS DEL LANZAMIENTO, CONTINÚE PERFECCIONANDO Y MEJORANDO SU SITIO WEB EN FUNCIÓN DE LOS COMENTARIOS Y ANÁLISIS DE LOS USUARIOS.

Día16-20: Desarrollo marketing

A medida que pasa de establecer su negocio a atraer clientes activamente, desarrollar una estrategia de marketing integral se vuelve fundamental. Esta fase consiste en crear un plan que aumente la visibilidad, atraiga a su público objetivo e impulse las ventas de sus productos digitales. He aquí cómo abordar estos días cruciales.

1. ESTABLECER UN CALENDARIO DE CONTENIDO

- Planifique temas: según los intereses y puntos débiles de su audiencia, planifique publicaciones de blog, videos, contenido de redes sociales y cualquier otro tipo de contenido que atraiga e interactúe con clientes potenciales.

- Contenido de video: planifique y produzca contenido de video que pueda compartirse en su sitio web, redes sociales y YouTube. Los videos pueden incluir tutoriales de productos, miradas detrás de escena o contenido educativo relacionado con su nicho.

2. APROVECHAR LAS REDES SOCIALES

- Selección de plataforma: elija las plataformas de redes sociales donde su público objetivo sea más activo. Para comenzar, concéntrese en 2 o 3 plataformas, como Instagram, LinkedIn y Facebook.

- Publicación consistente: utilice herramientas de programación para mantener un cronograma de publicación consistente. Interactúe con su audiencia respondiendo a comentarios y mensajes.

- Anuncios en redes sociales: planifique campañas publicitarias específicas para promocionar sus productos digitales, lanzamientos especiales o eventos. Utilice opciones de orientación específicas de la plataforma para llegar a clientes potenciales de manera efectiva.

1. CREAR UNA LISTA DE CORREO ELECTRÓNICO

- Imanes de clientes potenciales: cree valiosos imanes de clientes potenciales (por ejemplo, plantillas, libros electrónicos o seminarios web gratuitos) para alentar a los visitantes del sitio web a registrarse en su lista de correo electrónico.

- Secuencia de bienvenida: desarrolle una secuencia de bienvenida por correo electrónico que presente a los nuevos suscriptores su marca y sus productos digitales, brindando valor y preparando el escenario para futuras ventas.

2. CAMPAÑAS DE CORREO ELECTRÓNICO

- Lanzamientos de productos: utilice el marketing por correo electrónico para informar a su lista sobre lanzamientos de nuevos productos, ofreciendo descuentos exclusivos o acceso temprano a los suscriptores.

- Actualizaciones periódicas: mantenga a sus suscriptores interesados con actualizaciones periódicas, información sobre la industria y contenido valioso relacionado con su nicho.

3. SEO Y PRESENCIA ONLINE

- SEO en la página: asegúrese de que cada página de su sitio web, especialmente las páginas de productos, esté optimizada para los motores de búsqueda, incluido el uso de palabras clave relevantes, meta descripciones y etiquetas alt para imágenes.

- SEO de contenido: el contenido de su blog debe optimizarse para clasificar las palabras clave relacionadas con su industria y productos digitales, lo que ayuda a generar tráfico orgánico.

TIPS PARA *éxito*

- ENFOQUE ANALÍTICO: UTILICE HERRAMIENTAS COMO GOOGLE ANALYTICS E INFORMACIÓN DE LAS REDES SOCIALES PARA REALIZAR UN SEGUIMIENTO DEL DESEMPEÑO DE SUS ESFUERZOS DE MARKETING, AJUSTANDO LAS ESTRATEGIAS EN FUNCIÓN DE LOS DATOS.

- COMENTARIOS DE LOS CLIENTES: INCORPORE LOS COMENTARIOS DE SU AUDIENCIA PARA PERFECCIONAR SUS MENSAJES Y TÁCTICAS DE MARKETING.

- FLEXIBILIDAD: ESTÉ PREPARADO PARA CAMBIAR SU ESTRATEGIA EN FUNCIÓN DE LO QUE FUNCIONE. EL MARKETING ES UN PROCESO CONTINUO DE APRENDIZAJE Y ADAPTACIÓN.

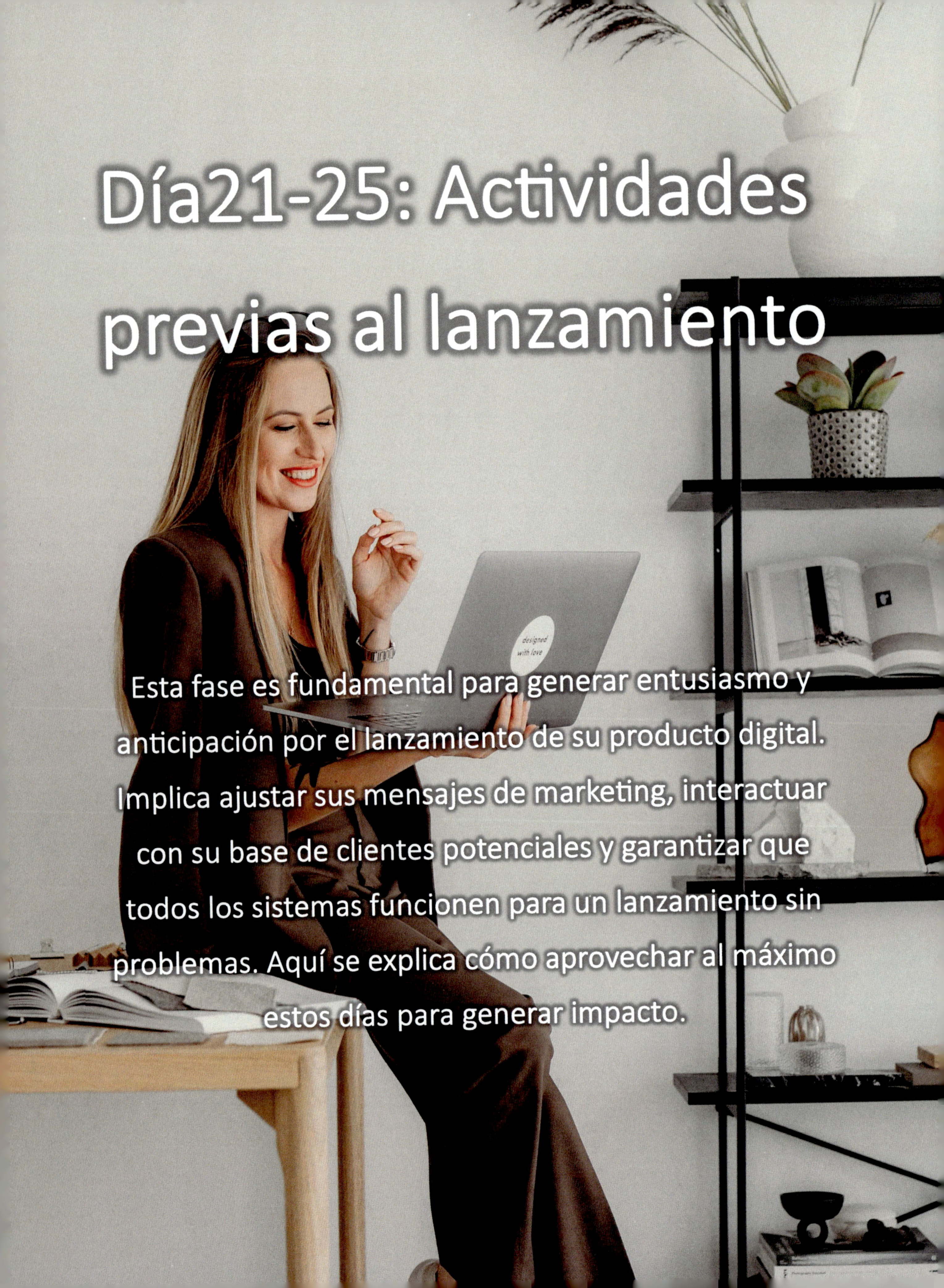

Día21-25: Actividades previas al lanzamiento

Esta fase es fundamental para generar entusiasmo y anticipación por el lanzamiento de su producto digital. Implica ajustar sus mensajes de marketing, interactuar con su base de clientes potenciales y garantizar que todos los sistemas funcionen para un lanzamiento sin problemas. Aquí se explica cómo aprovechar al máximo estos días para generar impacto.

1. CAMPAÑAS TEASER

- Avances de redes sociales: comparta adelantos, cuentas regresivas y videos de avance en las plataformas de redes sociales que elija para despertar la curiosidad y el entusiasmo.

- Adelantos por correo electrónico: envíe vistas previas exclusivas o miradas detrás de escena de su producto a su lista de correo electrónico, generando anticipación y haciendo que sus suscriptores se sientan especiales.

2. EVENTO DE LANZAMIENTO O SEMINARIO WEB

- Planifique un evento de lanzamiento: organice un evento de lanzamiento virtual o un seminario web para mostrar su producto digital. Esto podría incluir demostraciones en vivo, sesiones de preguntas y respuestas y ofertas especiales para los asistentes.

- Promoción: utilice su sitio web, redes sociales y lista de correo electrónico para promocionar el evento. Considere asociarse con personas influyentes u otras empresas para ampliar su alcance.

1. PRODUCTO POLACO

- Revisión final: revise su producto digital por última vez para verificar si hay errores o áreas de mejora. Asegúrese de que sea lo mejor posible antes de que se publique.

- Compras de prueba: realice compras de prueba para garantizar que el proceso de compra sea fluido. Compruebe que los sistemas automatizados de entrega de productos funcionen a la perfección.

2. OPTIMIZACIÓN DEL SITIO WEB

- Página de destino: cree una página de destino atractiva para su producto que destaque sus características, beneficios y cualquier oferta especial de lanzamiento.

- Experiencia de usuario: asegúrese de que su sitio web ofrezca una experiencia fluida e intuitiva para los visitantes. Verifique los tiempos de carga, la capacidad de respuesta móvil y la facilidad de navegación.

Involucrar a su audiencia

1. PARTICIPACIÓN EN LAS REDES SOCIALES

- Contenido interactivo: publique contenido interactivo como encuestas, cuestionarios o concursos relacionados con el lanzamiento de su producto para mantener a su audiencia interesada.

- Sesiones en vivo: organice sesiones en vivo en plataformas como Instagram, Facebook o YouTube para hablar sobre su producto, responder preguntas y conectarse con su audiencia.

2. COMPROMISO POR CORREO ELECTRÓNICO

- Correos electrónicos de cuenta regresiva: inicie una cuenta regresiva para el día del lanzamiento con correos electrónicos diarios o semanales que generen entusiasmo y compartan más información sobre su producto.

- Ofertas exclusivas: proporcione a sus suscriptores de correo electrónico ofertas o bonificaciones exclusivas si compran su producto durante el período de lanzamiento.

Los días 21 a 25 se dedican a aumentar el entusiasmo y garantizar que todo esté en su lugar para el lanzamiento exitoso del producto. Al interactuar con su audiencia, finalizar su producto y sitio web y generar anticipación a través de esfuerzos de marketing estratégico, prepara el escenario para una introducción exitosa de su producto digital en el mercado.

TIPS PARA *éxito*

- MENSAJES COHERENTES: ASEGÚRESE DE QUE TODAS LAS ACTIVIDADES PREVIAS AL LANZAMIENTO PRESENTEN MENSAJES COHERENTES SOBRE EL VALOR DE SU PRODUCTO Y LOS PROBLEMAS QUE RESUELVE.

- BUCLE DE RETROALIMENTACIÓN: UTILICE CUALQUIER RETROALIMENTACIÓN DE SUS ACTIVIDADES PREVIAS AL LANZAMIENTO PARA REALIZAR AJUSTES DE ÚLTIMO MOMENTO EN SU PRODUCTO O ESTRATEGIAS DE MARKETING.

- PREPARACIÓN TÉCNICA: VERIFIQUE TODOS LOS ASPECTOS TÉCNICOS RELACIONADOS CON EL LANZAMIENTO DE SU PRODUCTO, INCLUIDA LA FUNCIONALIDAD DEL SITIO WEB, EL PROCESAMIENTO DE PAGOS Y LOS MECANISMOS DE ENTREGA DEL PRODUCTO.

Día 26-lanzamiento y post lanzamiento

La culminación de su arduo trabajo, la fase de lanzamiento, es donde finalmente se lanza su producto digital. Este período es fundamental para aprovechar el impulso que ha creado y sentar las bases para un éxito sostenido. He aquí un enfoque detallado para estos últimos días y más allá.

Lanzamiento oficial

1. LANZAMIENTO OFICIAL

- Anuncio de lanzamiento: utilice todos sus canales (correo electrónico, redes sociales, su sitio web y cualquier asociación) para anunciar el lanzamiento. Hágalo claro, emocionante y atractivo.
- Ofertas especiales: considere ofrecer descuentos especiales el día del lanzamiento o por tiempo limitado para incentivar las compras inmediatas.
- Participe en tiempo real: sea activo en las redes sociales y en su sitio web para interactuar con los clientes, responder preguntas y agradecer a los compradores en tiempo real.

2. MONITOREO Y SOPORTE

- Seguimiento técnico: Esté atento a su sitio web y plataforma de ventas para detectar cualquier problema técnico que pueda obstaculizar el proceso de compra.
- Atención al cliente: ofrezca atención al cliente rápida y útil para abordar cualquier pregunta o problema que surja. Es más probable que los clientes satisfechos dejen críticas positivas y recomienden su producto a otros.

Recopilación de comentarios y testimonios

1. APROVECHANDO LOS TESTIMONIOS

- Encuestas: envíe encuestas a los clientes que hayan comprado su
- producto para recopilar comentarios sobre su experiencia y el producto en sí.
- Escucha social: supervise las redes sociales y los foros en línea en busca de menciones de su producto para recopilar comentarios y opiniones informales.

- Muestre reseñas positivas: utilice comentarios y testimonios positivos en sus materiales de marketing y en la página de su producto para generar confianza con los clientes potenciales.

Planificación para el crecimiento futuro

1. ANÁLISIS DE DATOS DE LANZAMIENTO

- Ventas y análisis: revise los datos de ventas y los análisis del sitio web para comprender el comportamiento del cliente, la efectividad de sus estrategias de marketing y las áreas de optimización.

- Comentarios de los clientes: recopile y analice los comentarios de los clientes para identificar temas, conocimientos y oportunidades comunes para mejorar el producto o desarrollar nuevos productos.

2. MARKETING Y DESARROLLO DE PRODUCTOS

- Marketing iterativo: basándose en los datos de su lanzamiento, refine su estrategia de marketing continua para llegar mejor y convertir a su público objetivo.

- Actualizaciones de productos y nuevos productos: planifique cualquier actualización de su producto actual en función de los comentarios o comience a conceptualizar nuevos productos que se alineen con su marca y las necesidades de sus clientes.

Los días 26 a 30 marcan no sólo el lanzamiento de su producto digital sino también el comienzo de su recorrido en el mercado. Al gestionar eficazmente las fases de lanzamiento y poslanzamiento, recopilar comentarios y actuar en función de ellos, y planificar el futuro, preparará su crecimiento y éxito continuos.

TIPS PARA *éxito*

- MANTÉNGASE COMPROMETIDO CON SU AUDIENCIA: CONTINÚE CONSTRUYENDO Y MANTENIENDO LA RELACIÓN CON SU AUDIENCIA A TRAVÉS DE ACTUALIZACIONES PERIÓDICAS, CONTENIDO VALIOSO Y PARTICIPACIÓN EN LAS REDES SOCIALES.

- APROVECHE LA RED Y LAS ASOCIACIONES: SIGA CONSTRUYENDO SU RED Y BUSQUE NUEVAS OPORTUNIDADES DE ASOCIACIÓN PARA AMPLIAR SU ALCANCE.

- REFLEXIONA Y APRENDE: TÓMATE EL TIEMPO PARA REFLEXIONAR SOBRE EL PROCESO DE LANZAMIENTO, OBSERVANDO QUÉ FUNCIONÓ BIEN Y QUÉ PODRÍA MEJORARSE PARA LA PRÓXIMA VEZ.

Made in the USA
Middletown, DE
04 September 2024

60352205R00071